Bead MEETS Metal

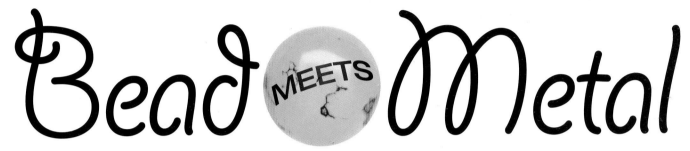

Easy metalwork techniques to showcase gemstone beads and other treasures

Kay Rashka

KB

KALMBACH BOOKS

Kalmbach Books
21027 Crossroads Circle
Waukesha, Wisconsin 53186
www.Kalmbach.com/Books

Please follow appropriate health and safety measures when working with materials and equipment. Some general guidelines are presented in this book, but always read and follow manufacturers' instructions.

Published in 2013
17 16 15 14 13   1 2 3 4 5

Manufactured in the United States of America

ISBN: 978-0-87116-440-7
EISBN: 978-0-87116-778-1

Editor: Mary Wohlgemuth
Art Director: Lisa Bergman
Technical Editor: Annie Pennington
Photographers: James Forbes, William Zuback

Library of Congress Cataloging-in-Publication Data

Rashka, Kay.
    Bead meets metal : easy metalwork techniques to showcase gemstone beads and other treasures / Kay Rashka.

    p. : col. ill. ; cm.

    Issued also as an ebook.
    ISBN: 978-0-87116-440-7

    1. Beadwork—Handbooks, manuals, etc. 2. Metal-work—Handbooks, manuals, etc.
    3. Jewelry making—Handbooks, manuals, etc. I. Title.

TT212 .R374 2013
745.594/2

CONTENTS

INTRODUCTION

I love beads! I really do. During the past 15 years, they stealthily started appearing in my metalworking studio. I enjoy the rainbow of colors, the varieties, the textures, the artistic shapes, and the history that so many of them carry. Whenever I travel, I seek out bead stores to bring home a few small bead mementos that I can easily carry in my handbag. I buy a bead I love, and then I design a piece of jewelry around it.

By incorporating these treasures in my work, I can wear them as miniature pieces of art. Learning metalworking techniques and merging wire and metal with my beads was the means to this end. With this book, I hope to share what I've learned and practiced in my 20 years as a metalsmith so you can turn your beads and other treasures into art jewelry too.

Buying mass-produced components such as bead caps, earring wires, and clasps can be costly and may limit your design options. By investing in some basic tools and learning some fundamental metalworking skills, you can customize your components to personalize your own bead-showcasing creations, increase their intrinsic value, and set your work apart from other designers' jewelry.

Kay Rashka

WHAT YOU WILL LEARN IN THIS BOOK

In this book, you'll learn about the tools and techniques that will take your jewelry-making skills to a new level. You will learn how to saw, form, drill, and texture sheet metal—techniques that are the foundation to making earrings, pendants, bead caps, charms, and other findings that make your jewelry special. You will learn which gauges of wire and sheet metal work well for your designs.

Many projects feature wirework, so you'll also learn how to form and forge wire to create earring wires and clasps. All of the projects incorporate a variety of gemstone beads or other found-object treasures. The projects that call for heat require only an easy-to-use, handheld butane torch, and you'll learn how to use it to ball wire ends and anneal and solder metal.

MATERIALS

Metal properties and measurement

Composition: Most of the designs in this book call for sterling silver or fine silver—these are considered **precious metals**. Some projects use nickel silver and copper—two common **base metals**, which are less expensive than precious metals.

Sterling silver is 92.5% silver and 7.5% other metal (usually copper). Jewelry made with sterling silver will tarnish with exposure to air because of the copper content. **Fine silver** is 99.99% silver and will not tarnish. It is very soft and malleable compared with sterling silver. **Nickel** is an alloy of 60% copper, 20% nickel, and 20% zinc. Although nickel is sometimes referred to as "nickel silver" and can be substituted for sterling silver, it contains no silver and can irritate some people's skin. **Copper** is 100% pure copper; it also causes reactions with certain people's skin.

Thickness (gauge) of wire and sheet metal: The thickness of wire and sheet metal is referred to as gauge. It is an inverse relationship: The thinner the metal, the larger the gauge number. For instance, 20-gauge wire is thinner than 18-gauge wire.

The gauge of wire or sheet can be measured with a handy bench tool called a **gauge plate**. Find the slot that fits the wire or sheet tightly and read the corresponding gauge of the metal on the plate. This book uses the Brown & Sharpe system (also known as the American Wire Gauge system) to identify gauge, which corresponds with how most metal and wire is measured and sold in the U.S.

Choosing gauge for projects: I choose the wire gauge for my earring hooks based on the size and style of the main earring component. A small, light earring design will work with 20-gauge wire. A larger, more pendulous earring might require thicker, 18-gauge wire.

Consider durability and weight as you choose the sheet metal gauge for a flat pendant or earring. For a small earring or pendant shape, consider 24- or 26-gauge metal. A medium or large pendant would probably look good cut from thick 20-gauge sheet. As you move into the projects, you'll find gauge recommendations for other techniques such as etching and using a disk cutter.

Hardness/temper: Metal has a crystalline structure. As you work metal by twisting, hammering, or shaping, its crystalline structure changes. During this process, called work-hardening, the metal's crystals break apart and become smaller, and the wire or sheet becomes harder and stiffer. At the extreme, if it is hammered too much, the metal will become so brittle and thin that it will likely break. Annealing is the opposite process of work-hardening: By applying heat, you relax and recrystallize the structure, and the metal softens and becomes more flexible.

You will often have a choice in temper when buying metal: dead-soft, half-hard, or hard. Dead-soft is the most flexible and easiest to form, and hard-rated metal is the stiffest. I usually purchase dead-soft sheet metal and dead-soft or half-hard sterling silver wire. Fine-silver sheet or wire is always considered to be dead soft, and thus needs to be forged or lightly hammered to add the stiffness required to hold a specific shape.

Wire profile: The most common wire profile is round. If another profile such as square is needed for a project, it will be noted in the materials list.

Buying metal: Precious metals are commodities traded on the open market, and prices fluctuate daily. Metal is sold in sheets or strips, usually with one dimension of the sheet fixed by the retailer. A common offering is 6" in one dimension; you determine the other flat dimension; for example, you might order a piece of 20-gauge sterling sheet in a 6x2" strip or a 6x12" sheet.

T I P Save scrap silver—every scrap of sheet or wire end trimming—for resale back to a supplier or metal refinery. Even filings can be saved and refined.

Other materials

Beads: Costarring with the metal in my jewelry are beads, of course. Most projects call for focal beads made of semiprecious gemstones. You'll also need a range of supporting-cast beads: some gemstone beads as well as beads made of other materials such as glass and metal.

Measurement conventions

Jewelry measurements don't follow a single standard convention. Beads are typically measured in millimeters; the measurement is end to end through the channel of the bead hole. Most professional jewelers use the metric system of millimeters and centimeters.

I use both metric and Imperial measurements in this book, with my choice based on the nature of the item or the precision needed in the measurement.

To convert inches to millimeters, multiply by 25.4. To find an inch equivalent of a measurement given in millimeters, multiply the number by 0.03937.

Insert a piece of sheet metal or wire into the slot on the gauge that seems close to the same width. Read the number on the slot that gives a tight fit.

WORKSPACE SAFETY

The first step in ensuring physical safety is recognizing that you risk getting hurt every time you pick up a tool. Some safety precautions are obvious, such as the need to wear eye protection when working with any power or rotary tool. But other safe practices are subtle, such as the proper way to dispose of a chemical solution used to antique metal.

As we age, it is likely that we need be close to a small project to see details as we work. This places our eyes at a greater risk of injury and adds to the risks of inhaling various materials.

For the sake of brevity, I do not repeat these safety guidelines throughout the book, although I call your attention to a particular caution when a tool or technique is introduced in the projects.

Please protect yourself and follow these safety guidelines for every piece of jewelry you make. Address safety issues before starting a project and develop good habits to ensure you'll be safe every time you begin a project.

SAFETY GUIDELINES

• **Wear a disposable dust mask** when using rotary tools that involve grinding or polishing. This will help protect you from breathing the metal dust generated as well as the fine, airborne particulate powder created as the tips and wheels you use begin to wear down.

• **Use adequate ventilation** whenever working with chemical solutions and when soldering.

• **Wear safety glasses** to protect your eyes from accidental chemical splashes as well as from broken drill bits or pieces of metal that might fly out of your hands while using a rotary tool. Standard prescription glasses are not considered safety glasses. You can find hard plastic safety glasses that will fit over your prescription glasses at most hardware stores.

• **Understand your supplies.** A number of chemical solutions are used to clean metal after soldering and to add color to metal surfaces. Take the time to understand the chemical composition of the liquid, what to do if you accidentally splash it on your skin, and how to safely dispose of it when needed. Always read the MSDS (Materials Safety Data Sheet) for any chemical you bring into your studio and keep a copy for future reference.

• **Understand the risks of handling compressed gas canisters.** Every torch uses some form of compressed gas. Regardless of the type of gas, these containers can explode when mishandled. Review your local fire ordinances and make sure that there are no prohibitions for having compressed gas in your living space. You may want to consult with your insurance agent as well.

• **Keep a fire extinguisher nearby** whenever working with open flames. Set up a heatproof work surface or station. Do not work with flame in a carpeted area.

• **Use grounded electrical outlets** and heavy-duty, grounded power cords with power tools. For projects requiring a rotary tool to drill beads or stones in a small dish of water, use an electrical outlet that is certified GFCI (ground fault circuit interrupter), which will cut power to the tool if a short circuit occurs.

• **Always tie back long hair,** and do not wear loose clothing when working with a torch or power tools. Wear clothes made of natural fibers to help minimize risks.

FABRICATION
tools & techniques

What does it mean to fabricate a piece of metal jewelry? Above all, it means that the jewelry is handmade, not cast or manufactured. Fabrication involves steps such as sawing, shaping, forming, joining, filing, and finishing, and these techniques require tools made specifically for jewelry making. It's important to have the right tools and know how to use them correctly and safely.

Fabrication tools

Most metalwork tools are one-time investments. Although acquiring the tools and accessories described here may seem daunting at first, after you make the initial investment, you'll have everything you need to make jewelry. The best sources for these specialty tools are bead show vendors, online jewelry suppliers, and bead stores.

The kits described in this section correspond to specific techniques used in making a metal jewelry project. You'll see photographs and detailed descriptions of the key tools and accessories needed for each technique. Some specialty tools and instructions for using them are described in projects later in the book.

I've divided the tools you'll need into eight **fabrication** toolkits: Cutting, Filing, Drilling, Forging & Forming, Finishing, Antiquing, Etching, and Tube-Riveting.

The **torchwork** section that follows describes everything you'll need for techniques that use flame: balling wire ends, annealing, and soldering.

Some toolkit descriptions are followed by a short exercise designed to familiarize you with the tools and techniques right away. (Look for the "Hands On" sidebars with a gray background.) In these exercises, you will be creating jewelry pieces as well as components you can use in your work—earrings, charms, tube-riveted stones, and jump rings.

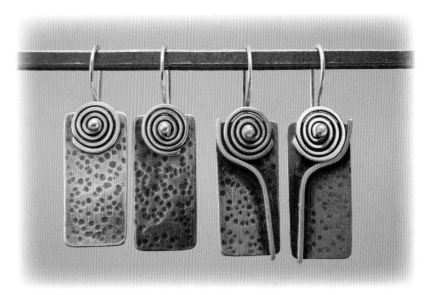

The Hands On exercises teach a variety of fabrication and torchwork techniques. These earrings are the results of some of the exercises. On the left is a pair made without torchwork; on the right is a soldered variation. The earrings are 3x14mm (rectangular section); total overall length 4.5cm.

Refer to these pages for information on the toolkits you'll need to complete the projects:

CUTTING

This is the toolkit used for cutting metal sheet, wire, and tubing using a jeweler's saw frame, wire cutters, metal-cutting shears, and disk cutters.

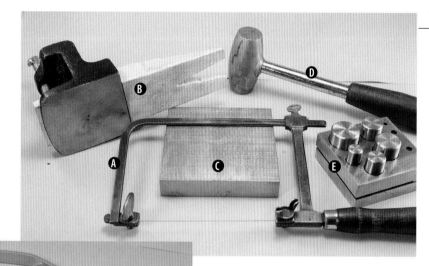

Sawing & disk cutting tools

A saw frame with blade
B bench pin with built-in block
C bench block
D brass mallet
E disk cutter

YOU'LL ALSO NEED:

(not pictured)

• Saw blade assortment (1/0 to 6/0)
• Wood dowels (various diameters)
• Rawhide mallet
• Blade lubricant: beeswax, Bur-Life, or mineral oil
• Leather scrap
• Fine-tip permanent markers
• Wire/sheet gauge
• Micrometer or ruler

Cutting tools

A fine-tip kitchen shears
B flush wire cutters
C heavy-duty wire cutters
D heavy-duty sheet-metal shears

Sawing metal

To saw a piece of metal, you'll need a jeweler's saw frame, saw blades, and a support called a bench pin.

Bench pin: The wood bench pin is two-sided and reversible: The flat side, which you'll use most often, is for sawing and general work support, and the angled side is used for filing and sanding. Some bench pins have a built-in steel block for forging (my preference, because it does double duty). Some bench pins are sold without a V slot; you can cut out this notch quite easily using a small wood handsaw or a hacksaw. Use wood-grade sandpaper to smooth any rough edges in the notch.

Saw blade: Saw blade teeth are unidirectional: The teeth point down and away from the saw frame when the

blade is properly inserted, so the blade cuts only on the downstroke. To saw thick metal, use a saw blade with large teeth.

Waxing: Before the first cut, run a piece of beeswax (or other lubricant) along the back of the blade. The sawing action generates enough heat to melt the wax and lubricate the teeth. If the blade catches, it's a sign the teeth are wearing

and it's time to change the blade. An assortment of blades from 1/0 to 6/0 will work for metal thicknesses from 20-gauge to 26-gauge, the gauges used in the projects. The recommended blade size is specified in each project; as a general guide, choose a saw blade size that has two or three teeth within the thickness of the metal you're cutting.

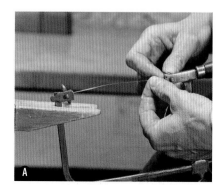

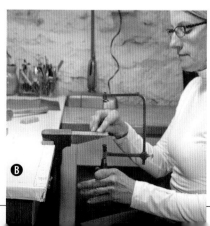

MORE HELPFUL HINTS FOR SAWING

Saw blade teeth: Avoid sawing fully out to either the top or bottom end of the saw blade where there are no teeth, or the blade will catch.

Shapes with corners vs. round shapes: When sawing sections with straight edges and corners, move only the saw frame forward along the outline. After a corner is cut, pick up the metal and reposition it on the bench pin. When sawing round shapes or curves, rotate the metal constantly toward the saw blade as it cuts; the saw frame stays in place at the edge of the bench pin.

Broken saw blades: If a blade breaks, just pull the portion still in the frame away from the metal piece and insert a new blade into the frame. Use a sawing motion to move the new blade through the cut line back to the position where the blade broke.

Outlines wear off: If the marker lines wear off due to pressure from your fingers, remove the saw by moving the blade backward through the cut section and retrace the pattern. You can also use a metal scribe to incise the lines on the metal.

Inserting the blade into a frame: Brace the frame between your body and a table edge with the open side of the frame pointing up and the handle pressed into your sternum. Loosen the blade wing nuts. Hold the saw blade with the teeth pointing up and insert the top end of the blade into the top wing nut. The teeth should point toward the handle. Tighten the top wing nut. Lean your body into the handle to compress the opening, insert the base of the blade into the lower wing nut, and tighten **[A]**. To test if the blade is tight, pluck it like a guitar string. If you hear a high-pitched "ping," the blade is at the correct tension. If you hear a "thud," it's too loose; reload the blade tighter.

Posture: Sit a few inches lower than what would normally feel comfortable for the table height. If you saw left-handed, sit to the right of the bench pin **[B]** and vice versa if you are right-handed. This position allows your elbow and forearm to move freely and keeps your arm in line with the bench pin.

Hand grip: Using a saw frame is all about holding the handle with a light touch. This technique takes some practice to perfect, so be patient. Hold the handle loosely between your thumb and index finger. Use your pinky finger to lightly brace the bottom of the handle **[C]**. Extend the other two fingers. If you're having trouble, pretend you're holding a baby's hand instead of a saw frame. You'll be surprised at how smooth the results are!

First cut: Practice sawing a straight line drawn onto a piece of metal. With the bench pin positioned with its flat side up, place the metal on the bench pin and hold the saw blade at a 45-degree angle to the metal edge **[D]**. With a loose grip, gently pull the handle back and down toward the floor behind you, allowing the teeth to cut into the metal. After the teeth cut into the metal, straighten the saw frame **[E]**. After the initial cut, always keep the handle vertical. Move the saw frame up and down to continue cutting the metal, letting the blade do the work.

Piercing: Sometimes you'll need to saw an interior shape out of a piece of metal; this is called piercing. To pierce, drill a hole in the center of the area to be removed with a #60 drill bit (see Drilling, p. 13). Secure the top of the saw blade into the frame and thread the saw blade through the hole. (If the hole is too small for the blade, enlarge it with a round needle file or drill again with a larger bit.) Secure the bottom of the blade in the frame and saw out the shape.

Other cutting tools

Wire cutters: Use high-quality super-flush wire cutters for cutting wire thinner than 18-gauge, and a pair of heavy-gauge cutters for thicker wire. To make a flush cut, place the flat side of the blades toward the end you want to be flush.

Shears: Kitchen shears (Joyce Chen brand or similar) are handy for cutting 22-gauge and thinner metal. Heavy-duty shears, as found in the sheet metal sections of large home-improvement stores, can cut metal thicker than 22-gauge in straight lines.

C

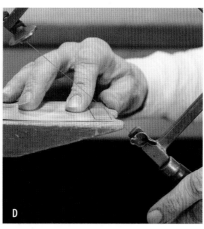

D

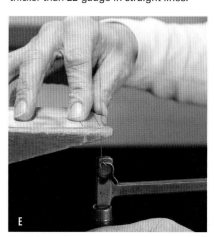

E

hands on: SAWING

Outline the shapes: Use a fine-tip permanent marker to trace two 14x29mm rectangles onto the metal. Leave a minimum of 2–3mm between the outline and the edge of the metal.

Saw the shapes: Place the metal on one side of the bench pin. Make the first cut and straighten the saw frame to vertical. Support most of the traced shape over the wood and not centered in the V-notch to avoid bending the metal. Align side 1 with the straight edge of the bench pin. Saw just outside of the outline **[A]** to help ensure that the final shape is not too small. (Most left-handed people saw a pattern out in a clockwise motion and vice versa for righties.) Continue sawing until the flat back of the saw blade just clears the first corner **[B]**.

To turn a corner: At the corner of side 1, keep the blade moving slowly up and down and start to turn just the saw frame. Do not move the metal. Move the blade slowly up and down without any forward movement: Think of it as marching in place. Continue sawing in place until the

saw frame is fully turned 90 degrees away from you **[C]**. Do not turn the frame unless the blade is sawing up and down to avoid breaking the blade. (Technical note: Some instructors teach a different technique for turning corners, but this method has proven itself in many years of practice for me and my students.)

Pick up the metal with the blade in place at corner 1. Do not remove the blade from the metal. Position the metal and the saw blade so side 2 is aligned with the edge of the bench pin **[D]**. Notice that the portion of the rectangle being cut is on top of the bench pin. Continue sawing the remaining sides and corners in this way.

Test the metal shape for flatness: If you plan to texture the metal later, it is not necessary to test for flatness. If you plan to solder onto the metal, it needs to be absolutely flat. These earrings will be textured, but here's the process to practice testing for flatness: Place a piece of 320- or 400-grit sandpaper on a flat surface. Sand both sides of the metal using a figure-8 motion. This removes burrs left on the edge from sawing and starts to create a uniform surface finish. If there are uneven spots in the metal, such as at a corner, the sanding finish will not be uniform. Place the metal on a bench block, strike it firmly with a rawhide mallet several times, and sand again. ∎

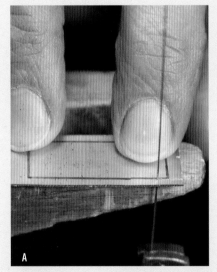

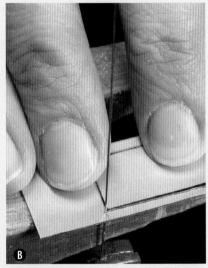

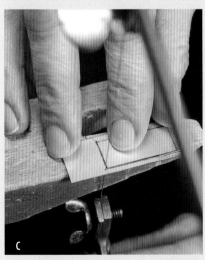

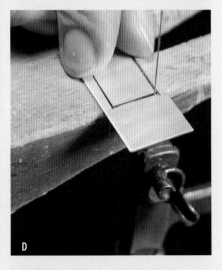

NEXT STEP: File the edges of the rectangles (p. 12)

The cutting face of a punch (left) and the striking face (right). The disk cutter base is in the background.

Using a disk cutter

I use a lot of disks in my jewelry—for spacers and bead caps, in particular. Disks are easily cut out using a jeweler's saw, but if you need small disks (10mm diameter or smaller), it is much quicker and easier to use a disk cutter.

Disk cutters are designed for metal sheet up to 24-gauge. (Use a saw for thicker metal.) They produce disks ranging from tiny (6mm) to about 25mm in diameter. The cutting cylinders are called punches. Each punch has a cutting edge, which contacts the metal, and a beveled striking edge, which you hit with a mallet or hammer. The metal will cut more easily and the punches will last longer if you anneal the metal before punching to soften it (see Annealing, p. 35) and lubricate the punch for each cut.

Mallet: A wide-faced, heavy mallet or dead-blow hammer works best. You want to cut the disk with one powerful strike, so the heavier the mallet, the better.

Size of sheet metal: For jewelry projects, I usually work with a narrow strip of metal—just a few millimeters wider than the punch is wide enough, providing that you position the metal carefully.

Cutter workstation: An ideal surface is a solid, uncarpeted floor because a table surface is likely to flex with the force of the hammer. Placing the block on the floor allows you to leverage the weight of your upper body downward. I use a standard metal bench block covered by a piece of leather under the cutter. The leather protects the bench block from the impact and protects the disk as it drops down.

Safety: Wear safety glasses. Place the heel of your hand on the cutter block with fingers pointed away from the punch.

Cutting a disk: Use a paper towel to wipe a light coating of lubricant over the cutting face of the punch. Insert and center the strip of metal between the plates of the cutter below the cutting hole with about 2–3mm of metal surrounding the cutting hole. Place the cutting end into the hole and rest it on the metal strip. Strike the top of the punch squarely with the mallet [A]. The disk should cut and push down to the leather. Remove the disk. (Be careful when handling the sharp edges of the metal salvage after cutting the disks.)

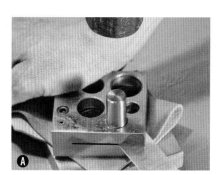

Use flush cutters to trim any small, sharp bits along the edge [B]. Use a piece of 220-grit silicon carbide sandpaper to smooth any remaining burrs. Next, use finer grades of sandpaper to sand and polish the disk surfaces. The disk edges can be polished using either a fine or extra-fine polishing wheel (see Finishing, p. 18).

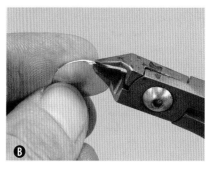

Stuck punch: Occasionally a punch will get caught in a cutter along the edge of the metal salvage. First try to loosen the metal and the punch by moving the metal back and forth; the punch usually loosens. If not, prop the cutter over a table edge. Place a stack of newspapers or something soft below to catch the punch as it falls out to prevent damage. Place a wood dowel on top of the punch and strike it lightly with a hammer [C]. The punch should easily fall out.

FILING

The sharp, parallel teeth of jewelry files are used to smooth rough metal edges and for detail shaping. Files cut only on the push stroke with the file moving away from you. Use a long stroke, not short movements, and always hold metal against a bench pin.

File characteristics

The cut of the file refers to how fine its teeth are. Hand files for jewelry making include large, coarse hand files for quickly removing metal on the first pass as well as small, thin needle files for precision work. For a more comfortable grip on the file, purchase a handle and insert the tang of the file into the handle.

Hand files are identified by a number indicating how fine the cutting surface is: A #1 file is coarser than a #2 file, for example. Match the shape of the file to the contour of what you are filing. A flat-faced or a half-round file will be most useful for a wide variety of jobs. If you purchase only one file to start, get a half-round file—it's good for flat and curved edges. Needle files are often sold in sets of 6 to 12 in a variety of shapes such as round, flat, triangle, half round, and square.

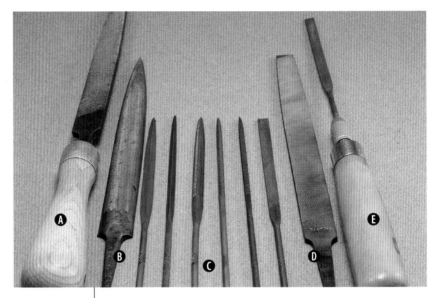

General-use files

A hand file with handle
B half-round hand file
C set of needle files
D flat hand file
E needle file with handle

hands on: FILING

TOOLKIT
• Filing

MATERIALS
• Metal rectangles from Hands On p. 10

Your rectangles are probably not yet the perfect shape. A coarse-cut hand file will quickly help you file and remove any imperfections in the shape. The cutting action of the file is always with the tang-to-tip (push) stroke. An easy way to file flat edges is to place a flat hand file on a

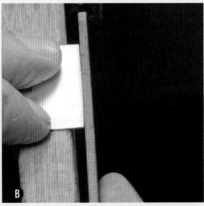

table, place the metal on its edge, and pull the metal across the file toward the tang **[A]**. Or, place the metal at the edge of the bench pin and file along the edge using the bench pin for leverage **[B]**. ■

NEXT STEP: Drill holes for the earring wires (p. 14)

DRILLING

Most jewelry makers use some type of power tool to drill holes in metal. As you begin, you'll find that a handheld rotary tool will do the job. As you progress, you may want to invest in a flex shaft, the choice of many professional jewelers. Both tools allow you to work with a variety of drill bits as well as other attachments for other fabrication tasks.

Rotary tools

Handheld rotary tool: Commonly used by hobbyists and woodworkers, handheld rotary tools can be found in most hardware stores (Dremel is a well-known brand). At the tip of the unit is a collet that secures a drill bit or other attachment. You can add a chuck that allows quick changes among tips. A variable-speed unit is the most versatile and useful for metalwork.

Flex shaft: A flex shaft is another type of motorized rotary tool. Unlike the handheld tool, the motor of the flex shaft is separate from the handpiece and can be hung from a hook above your workbench. The shaft is about three feet long and contains a spinning cable that activates the drill bit or other attachment held in the handpiece. You control the speed with a foot pedal.

Rotary tools can be used with a multitude of polishing, cutting, and grinding tips. These tools operate at high speeds, so please follow the manufacturer's safety recommendations.

Other piercing & drilling tools

Drill bits: Most metal jewelry projects require the use of thin, **high-speed twist drill bits** identified by numbers. I use a #60 bit to drill holes for 18- and 20-gauge earring wires; I suggest you buy an assortment of sizes from #50–#70. You may find these fine bits at a large hardware store, but more commonly they are found online. A lower number correlates to a larger-diameter bit. Use beeswax or a commercial lubricant to extend the life of the bit before each hole is drilled.

Super-hard and durable **carbide drill bits** are effective for drilling large holes in metal for setting wire and tube rivets; buy a range of sizes from 2–5mm.

Basic drilling tools
A Flex shaft with #30 handpiece
B utility hammer
C rotary hand tools
D bench block
E beeswax
F carbide drill bit
G automatic center punch
H center punch
I set of high-speed twist drill bits
J screw-action hole punch

YOU'LL ALSO NEED:
(not pictured)
- Diamond drill bit assortment
- Small pieces of leather
- Beeswax or commercial lubricant
- Permanent markers
- Dremel chuck #4486
- Safety accessories: safety glasses, dust masks, GFCI outlets

To drill stones, glass, and ceramic, use **diamond-coated drill bits**. For the projects in this book, get 1mm and 1.5mm straight-shaft diamond-coated bits and a range of hollow-core diamond-coated bits from 2.5–6.5mm. Use these bits with water as a lubricant and to wash away material as it is drilled. A **tapered diamond-coated drill bit** is helpful to begin enlarging bead holes.

Center punch: A center punch is used to put a dimple in metal to guide a drill bit so it doesn't skate off the surface. Use a straight-shaft center punch with a hammer or a spring-loaded center punch.

Screw-action punch: These punches are handy but create only two sizes of holes—typically a 1/16" hole and a 3/32" hole, which correspond roughly to 14- or 15-gauge and 10- or 11-gauge wire. These punches work great for making a hole to fit a rivet or a jump ring. Save the waste pieces of metal to use as soldered embellishment.

Other forming & forging tools

A wood dapping block and punch

B two sizes of bench horn anvils

C steel dapping block and punches

D ring mandrel

E bezel mandrels in various profiles

Other forming & forging tools

Dapping punches and blocks: A dapping punch set includes punches with spherical ends and a dapping block with various sizes of half-dome depressions. Use a hammer to strike the dapping punch to form a piece of metal into the concave shapes of the dapping block.

For a shallow dome, a wood dapping block and punch is adequate. This style of dapping block works well for metals no thicker than 24-gauge. Thick metals will be easier to dome if they are annealed first to make them more pliable.

If a deep dome is desired, use a steel dapping block and steel punches. Steel dapping punches come in a variety of sizes that correspond to specific depressions in a dapping block. You'll need a range of punch sizes from about 5–14mm for the projects in this book. Note that steel blocks may distort lightly textured metal because steel is harder than the nonferrous metal.

Anvils and mandrels: These steel tools are usually used with a hammer or mallet to form sheet metal or wire into a specific shape, such as a ring. A horn anvil is a miniature version of the large bench

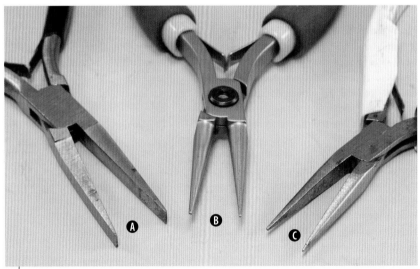

Jewelry pliers

A flatnose pliers

B roundnose pliers

C chainnose pliers

YOU'LL ALSO NEED:

(not pictured)
• Combination flatnose/half-round pliers

anvil; the horn is especially helpful for forming curved shapes.

Ring and bezel mandrels come in a variety of shapes and sizes (round, square, and triangular, for example), and in wood and plastic as well as steel. Use a round steel ring mandrel for the projects in this book.

Jewelry pliers (flatnose, roundnose, chainnose): Unlike hardware-store pliers, high-quality pliers for jewelry making have smooth inside jaws, improved ergonomic efficiency, and narrow tips that allow precise wire shaping. Some projects call for combination flatnose/half-round pliers, which is helpful for forming rings.

Texturing & stamping tools

These tools allow you to add your own design motifs to projects. Design stamps can be used in a specific pattern or randomly across metal. I like to use the ball-peen face of my chasing hammer to create a distressed look on metal.

Steel stamps: Artistic design and alphabet stamps are made of hard steel. You'll find alphabet stamps sold in sets in a variety of type styles. Design stamps are usually sold individually.

Rubber block: You can place a rubber block below a bench block to act as a sound deadener. Hammer texturing and stamping can get quite loud!

Steel bench block: Use a steel bench block under metal sheet or wire when forging or texturing. A wood block is too soft and will absorb the force of the hammer blows.

Utility hammer and brass-head mallet: Use either a heavy utility hammer or a brass-head mallet to strike stamps on metal. The brass-head mallet is often called a dead-blow mallet because its heavy head strikes the stamp with a lot of force and minimal rebound.

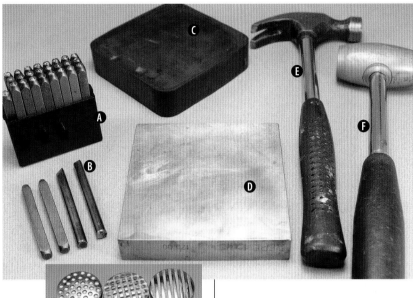

Texturing hammers: These hammers usually have a different texture on each face, and some have removable, interchangeable faces. The faces are slightly domed, but be careful as you use them so they don't nick or distort the edges of the metal.

Texturing & stamping tools

A alphabet stamps
B design stamps
C rubber block
D steel bench block
E utility hammer
F brass-head mallet
G texturing hammers

hands on:
TEXTURING

TOOLKIT
• Forming & Forging

MATERIALS
• Metal rectangles from Hands On p. 14

I textured my earrings using a chasing hammer. You can try this texture or create a pattern using a design stamp across the surfaces of the rectangles for your earrings.

Texture the rectangles: Place each rectangle on a bench block with a thick rubber block below. Strike the metal lightly with the ball-peen end of a chasing hammer **[A]**. If the rectangle cups upward due to the texturing, flatten it by striking it with a rawhide mallet.

Stamp the surfaces: Place the design end of the stamp squarely over the metal rectangle on a bench block. Place the side of your hand on the block for leverage and stability. Rock the stamp back and forth to get a feel for when the end of the stamp is sitting flat on the metal. Use a heavy utility hammer or brass mallet to strike the top of the stamp squarely. Try not to move as the hammer strikes the stamp. If the stamp rocks at all, you will get only a partial impression, which is

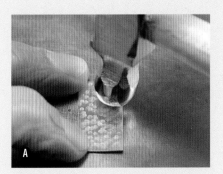

nearly impossible to fix. Flatten the metal with a rawhide mallet if necessary. ■

NEXT STEP: Finish the surfaces and edges (p. 21)

FINISHING

Attention to finishing is a trademark of high-quality artisan jewelry. Look closely at a pair of earrings you may have purchased at an art fair. Are the edges and corners smoothed and rounded? Are all flat metal surfaces finished uniformly without scratches? Are the earring wires handmade? If so, they probably have no stray tool marks. Even the back of the piece looks as finished as the front. Finishing techniques can be performed by hand or with rotary tools and tips.

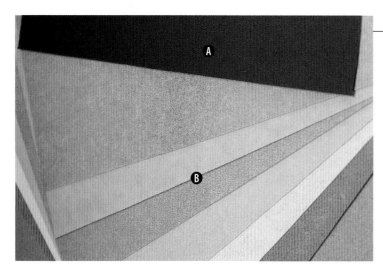

Finishing papers

A silicon carbide sandpaper

B assortment of polishing papers

YOU'LL ALSO NEED:
(not pictured)
• Flat craft sticks

Sandpaper & polishing papers

Metalsmiths use a series of sanding papers rated by grit size. As the number gets larger, the grit gets finer. The coarser, lower-number grits such as 220 or 320 are useful for removing scratches and edge burrs. Finer grits such as 400 and 600 give metal surfaces a uniform finish. Always work from the coarsest grit necessary to the finest, and don't skip any steps between. Sand in one direction to remove deep scratches. With the next-finest grit, sand in a different direction until you remove all the marks left by the coarser grit.

Silicon carbide sandpaper: This black or gray sandpaper can be purchased at most hardware stores; get a range from 180- to 600-grit. This sandpaper is more durable than micron-graded finishing paper, and it can be used wet or dry. The coarse 180- and 220-grit papers are useful for removing burrs and deep scratches; use the medium 320-grit and finer 400- and 600-grits to smooth surface blemishes and create a satin finish. Cut the paper

into 4x4" squares to make it easy to work with, and record the grit on the back of each piece.

Micron-graded polishing papers: Working with polishing paper is cleaner than using sandpaper. These papers are soft and cloth-like, which allows them to conform to uneven and dimensional surfaces. I am a big fan of 3M Tri-M-Ite papers, available in a variety of color-coded grits from coarse (400-grit/30μ) to extra-fine (8000-grit/1μ). I primarily use 400-grit (yellow-green), which creates a satin luster on silver. Polishing paper has a more-uniform abrasive particle size than silicon carbide paper, so the finishes imparted to metal are also more uniform.

Rotary tool accessories

Rubberized abrasive polishing tips: These tips are made from a rubberized compound that contains silicon carbide polishing grit: They are basically sandpaper on a spinning mandrel. They are available in three shapes: wheels, knife-edge wheels, and bullets. I use these primarily to finish, polish, and bevel

edges. Don't use them to polish flat metal surfaces; they will leave uneven marks.

Four different grits are available; I recommend using the rust-colored tips (fine grit) and the gray/green tips (extra-fine). A coarse tip will remove metal quickly, and the extra-fine and fine tips are good all-purpose accessories.

To create a handy sanding or polishing stick, wrap a small piece of 320-grit sandpaper or 400-grit polishing paper around a craft stick.

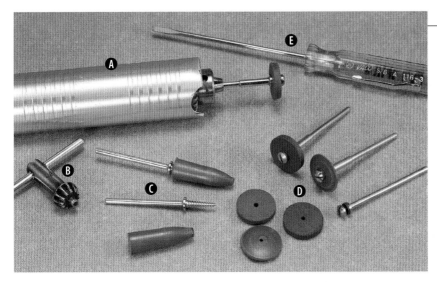

Finishing tools

A handpiece with chuck

B chuck key

C rubberized bullet tips and threaded mandrels

D rubberized wheel tips and screw mandrels

E eyeglass screwdriver

F radial bristle disks

G polishing compound and felt polishing tips

YOU'LL ALSO NEED:
(not pictured)
- Dremel chuck #4486 for rotary tool
- Cup burs (various sizes, 1.8mm–2.5mm)
- Superfine (0000) steel wool
- Liquid dish soap
- Jewelry polishing cloth
- Microcrystalline wax

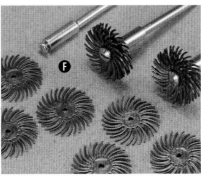

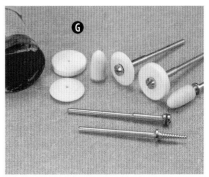

The wheels come in various diameters up to 1". The ⅝" wheel is the most effective for polishing and light grinding the type of jewelry I make because of its narrow diameter. The knife-edge wheels work great for getting into tight spaces. The wheels are mounted on screw mandrels for use with a rotary tool. Use an eyeglass repair screwdriver for tightening the set screw on the mandrels.

The bullet tips are mounted on threaded point mandrels. They are useful for polishing small surfaces (1–2mm wide), flattened wire, metal edges, and the insides of rings and earring hooks.

Add a Dremel chuck #4486 to your rotary hand tool for quick changes of bits and tips—it eliminates the need for a collet.

Radial bristle disks: These flexible abrasive bristle wheels, made by 3M, come in a range of grits from 36-grit to 1 micron. The red (220-grit) and blue (400-grit) wheels are the most useful

for my projects. They can be used to remove discoloration that occurs during soldering, to create a uniform satin surface finish, and to clean metal after etching. They work very well to access hard-to-reach areas for uniform polishing. A fine-grit wheel can leave a uniform satin finish. Use at least three wheels at once on a screw mandrel, oriented so the brush tips are on the leading edge of the rotary tool's spin.

Felt polishing tips: When used with polishing compounds such as red rouge or Fabulustre, these rotary tool tips will polish metal surfaces to a bright, mirror-like finish (assuming you have done some prep work with sandpaper to remove scratches). The tips are made of a dense material similar to wool. They are available as wheels, knife-edge wheels, and bullets. The bullet tips work well to polish the inside of round shapes such as rings and earring wires. The tips are rated as hard, medium, and soft; I use the hard felt tips to polish edges and the soft felt tips for broader surfaces.

To polish with a felt wheel, mount the wheel on a ¹⁄₁₆" screw mandrel and tighten the mandrel in the chuck. Turn the unit on at a slow speed and touch the wheel to the surface of the polishing compound. Use the wheel to polish the surfaces and the edges of the metal, moving the wheel around until the metal has a mirror-like finish. Apply more polishing compound as needed. The metal will get hot, so stop to let it cool as necessary. Wash the metal with soapy water to remove the polishing compound, rinse, and dry.

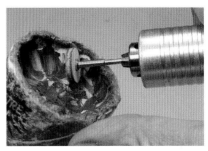

Using a slow speed, lightly brush the wheel in the polishing compound.

YOU'LL ALSO NEED:

(not pictured)

• Stainless steel shot

• Burnishing compound or liquid dish soap

Use about ¾ cup of shot, water to cover, and a drop of burnishing compound, and place the metal items in the barrel.

Rotary tumbler

As an option, a single- or double-barrel rotary tumbler can be used to polish metal surfaces of jewelry to a bright, shiny finish—everything from small, semiprecious metal items such as charms and pendants to delicate items such as forged metal earrings and necklace chains. For the small investment, these tumblers are a powerful time-saver, especially if you find you are creating a lot of jewelry. Before you tumble items, finish the surfaces uniformly and remove all nicks and scratches. (Do not tumble-polish soft gemstones such as opal or turquoise.)

For a 3 lb. tumbler barrel, add about ¾ cup of stainless steel shot and water to a height about ½" higher than the shot level. Add a drop of commercial burnishing compound or liquid dish soap. Place the metal items in the barrel, insert the rubber lid, and tighten the lock nut. Place the barrel on its side on the tumbler.

Run the tumbler for about 30 minutes and check your items. If the metal is polished and shiny enough, rinse well and dry. If not, continue tumbling. I use a long-handled kitchen strainer to drain the shot and sort through to find my items. Rinse the stainless shot and the barrel, and let the shot dry before storing.

Other finishing accessories

Cup bur: A cup bur can be used by hand or on a rotary tool—it's a quick way to smooth the ends of wire and is especially handy for finishing earring wires. As you rotate the cupped end around a wire end, the fine teeth inside smooth the end. Buy cup burs in sizes to match the wire gauges you use most often. Use a cup bur that is slightly larger than wire end; for 18-gauge wire, I use a 2.3mm diameter cup bur.

Steel wool: Use superfine (0000) steel wool to give metal surfaces a satin finish. Place the metal on a bench block and buff it with a small piece of steel wool. Make sure the metal is completely dry; any residual moisture can create small rust spots if any steel fibers break off during the buffing.

Liquid dish soap: A final step in finishing is washing your piece in soapy water to clean off all residue. Add a drop or two of liquid soap to a little warm water in a cup or sink, brush the piece with a soft-bristle brush, rinse in clear water, and dry.

Polishing cloth: Buff pieces with a jewelry polishing cloth after the surfaces have been finished to remove tiny scratches and nicks. The polishing cloth is treated with a chemical that will help protect the jewelry.

Microcrystalline wax: This final finish is helpful for preserving color added with solutions such as liver of sulfur or other patina products. Carnauba car wax or spray-on lacquer can also be used.

hands on: FINISHING

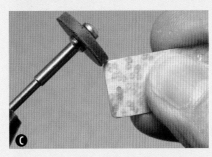

Remove edge marks: Although you filed the edges of the rectangles, they may still show some saw marks. Tighten a ⅝" diameter extra-fine or fine-grit abrasive wheel to a ¹⁄₁₆" diameter screw mandrel [A]. Place the wheel on the edge of the piece of metal. Use a fairly slow motor speed and a gentle off-and-on motion to move the wheel along the edge of the piece [B]. Don't hold the wheel in constant contact with the metal; it will grind a groove into the wheel and reduce its effectiveness.

Smooth sharp corners and tips: Slow the speed of the rotary tool and use a back-and-forth motion on the corner until it rounds out and you see no nicks or blemishes around the whole perimeter [C].

Bevel the edges: Even after you smooth the metal edges, you can add one more finishing step: bevel or round off the edges (although because the metal is quite thin, the effect of beveling will be subtle). Orient the extra-fine grit wheel perpendicular to and slightly over the edge [D].

Using a slow speed and keeping the wheel in this orientation, move it slowly around the edge of the whole piece, including the corners. The wheel may leave some marks at the edge of the metal. Repeat this process on the back. Sand both sides again with medium to fine-grit sandpaper to remove the wheel marks. Run your fingers along the edge of the metal to feel how smooth and rounded it feels.

Sand and finish: Any residual surface scratches and nicks can be removed using 320-grit sandpaper or 400-grit polishing paper. Place the paper on a flat, clean, hard surface such as a bench block or a tabletop. Lay the metal face down on a clean section of the paper. Sand the metal back and forth across the paper in a uniform, straight motion. It is easier to stand while sanding to allow your whole arm and shoulder to work in the effort.

Look at the sanded surface. Are all the original scratches removed? Do you want a smoother finish? If so, continue with a progression of finer grits until you no longer see the marks of the previously used paper. Sand both sides of each metal piece. For effective sanding, work on a clean or unused area as the paper shows use. If you've used sandpaper, wash the metal with soapy water to remove any grit. Rinse with water and dry with a soft cloth. ∎

MORE HELPFUL HINTS FOR FINISHING

Polishing and beveling metal edges without using power tools: If you don't have access to a rotary tool, use a sanding stick or a needle file to make metal edges uniform and polished.

Removing stubborn scratches: If a scratch won't sand out, try a piece of coarse sandpaper such as 220-grit. Move the metal back and forth in a straight motion across the paper. Pick up the metal, rotate it 90 degrees, and sand again in the new orientation. Repeat this rotational/sanding process until the scratch disappears. After the surface looks uniform, progress through finer-grit sandpapers for the final finish.

NEXT STEP: Form the spirals (p. 22)

hands on:
FORMING SPIRALS

TOOLKIT
• Forming & Forging

MATERIALS
• 18- or 20-gauge fine-silver wire (20–25cm)
• Rectangles from Hands On p. 21

Spirals can be either loosely or tightly wound. Tightly wound spirals are less likely to pull apart if they get caught on something. A four-revolution spiral made of 18-gauge fine-silver wire will use about 8cm of wire when forged and wound tightly to a finished diameter of about 1cm.

Cut the wire and forge the start of the spirals: Cut two 12–15cm pieces of 18- or 20-gauge fine-silver wire. Use the flat side of a needle file or a cup bur to round one end of each wire **[A]**. Turn a single revolution loop in this end of each wire using the tip of the chainnose pliers **[B]**. Test that 20-gauge wire (used for the earring wire later in this project) can fit though the loop and adjust the loop size if necessary. Place each loop on a bench block and lightly flatten it with a chasing hammer without striking the straight section of wire **[C]**. I protect the straight section of wire by placing my fingernail over the wire to keep the hammer from hitting it.

Form the spiral: With the nose of the chainnose pliers pointed up, place the loop in the jaws so the tail extends from the bottom of the spiral to the left at the 9 o'clock position **[D]**. The jaws are firmly grasping the loop at 12 and 6. Use your thumb to push the tail from 9 o'clock to about 11 **[E]**. Reposition the wire in the jaws again so the tail is to the left of the pliers at 9 **[F]**. Use your thumb to push the wire to about 11 again. Repeat this process to add one full revolution of wire.

Flatten the spiral: Use the wide, domed face of the chasing hammer to lightly widen the outer revolution of wire. Avoid striking the straight part of the wire. Bring the hammer face squarely down on the edge of the spiral **[G]**. As the hammer face makes contact with the wire, finish the stroke off to the side in a brushing motion; the wire will widen in this direction.

Finish and trim the spiral: Place the forged spiral in the jaws of the chainnose pliers with the tail extending at 9. Repeat the turning and forging process one revolution at a time until the spirals are the desired size (about 3–5 revolutions). Trim the wire tail. Use the tip of a flat needle file or an abrasive wheel to smooth the tip of each spiral wire. Make two spirals.

If the spirals have any tool marks, polish them with an extra-fine abrasive wheel **[H]** or sand them on a piece of 320- or 400-grit sandpaper. Check the spirals for size by placing them on the rectangles **[I]**. ■

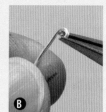

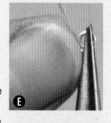
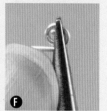

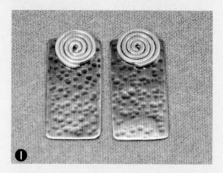

NEXT STEP: Make the earring wires (p. 23)

hands on:
MAKING EARRING WIRES

I use lightly forged fine-silver wire as well as sterling silver wire for earring wires. If you need a long earring wire, use sterling silver wire because it will keep its shape better due to its stiffness.

For each earring wire: Thread a balled wire through a spiral and the drilled hole of the metal rectangle, positioning the spirals as mirror images. Hold the wire tightly at the back of the metal piece using chainnose pliers. Bend the wire upward at a right angle **[A]**.

Thread a crimp bead onto the wire to sit where the pliers' jaws held the wire. Use the tip of the chainnose pliers to flatten the crimp bead to prevent the metal shapes from sliding up the earring wire **[B]**. Be sure the spiral can rotate freely.

Bend the wire forward and across the top of the metal shape **[C]**. Turn the earring so the spiral faces forward. Position a mandrel such as a wood dowel or a pen over the metal piece and touching the wire. Bend the wire tail back and around the mandrel to make the curved part of each earring wire **[D]**.

Adjust the shapes: Hang both earrings on a thin mandrel to check for even lengths. If the lengths are not the same, shorten the longer ear wire: Hold the mandrel against the earring wire loop and pull out some of the excess length. With your fingers, make a small outward bend in the wire near the bottom of the rectangle **[E]**. Use chainnose pliers to straighten any bends in the earring wires.

Forge the earring wires: Place the earring on a bench block with the metal shape hanging off the side. The earring wire should be lying on the edge of the bench block. Use the flat face of a riveting hammer to gently hammer the earring wire directly behind the back of the metal piece until it is lightly flattened **[F]**. Use care, because the hammer face can nick the wire if the hammer strikes are too hard. A chasing hammer face is too large to flatten the wire directly behind the rectangle.

As you move farther up the earring wire, use a half-dome chasing hammer to continue to flatten the wire toward the end. Do not make the wire too thin. This work-hardening will help the wire hold shape. Flip the wire over and lightly hammer the other side. The curved face of the chasing hammer is less likely to nick the wire than the riveting hammer.

Polish: Use a 400-grit polishing stick to smooth the earring wires and remove any hammer marks **[G]**. To polish and buff the underside of the earring wires, use an extra-fine-grit abrasive bullet to create a uniform surface finish **[H]**. If there are any nicks in the earring wire that are hard to polish with the buffing stick, use an extra-fine-grit abrasive knife-edge wheel to remove them **[I]**.

Smooth the ends: Flush-cut the end of each earring wire. Use a needle file to round off the end. You can also use a cup bur in a rotary tool or by hand. Place the wire end in the rotating cup bur to smooth it **[J]**. ∎

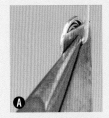
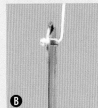
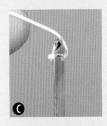

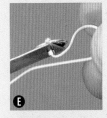
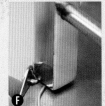
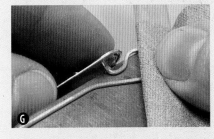
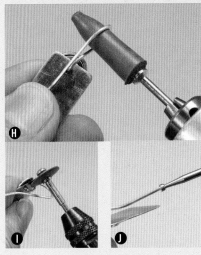

NEXT STEP: Antique the earrings (p. 24)

23

ANTIQUING with liver of sulfur

Compounds designed to add a colored finish (patina) to metal help texture really stand out. Liver of sulfur solution is my favorite way to add an aged look to many metals.

Liver of sulfur: Liver of sulfur is used to give an aged look to metal (thus I refer to this process in this book as antiquing). Liver of sulfur will darken copper, sterling silver, fine silver, brass, bronze, and nickel. It is available in chunks, liquid, and gel forms—all with a distinctive "rotten egg" smell. I usually use the chunk form, which must be dissolved in water and works fastest warm. You can also rinse the metal piece in hot water first to speed the reaction. Solution strength also affects how quickly the metal takes on color. Use liver of sulfur solution to antique copper, brass, sterling silver, and fine silver. Although liver of sulfur may work on nickel silver, you'll get better results with a solution made for nickel.

Antiquing is especially effective on textured pieces. After applying the

solution, remove some of the dark patina from the high surfaces of the metal by buffing with superfine steel wool or 400-grit polishing paper.

Antiquing tools & supplies

A superfine steel wool

B 400-grit polishing paper

C cotton swabs

D plastic tweezers

E liver of sulfur chunks

F microcrystalline wax

G liver of sulfur gel

H baking soda

I water dish

Sealing: A thin layer of microcrystalline wax or spray-on lacquer will preserve the look of patina on metal. You may need to reapply the patina and wax from time to time if the jewelry gets heavy wear.

hands on: ANTIQUING

TOOLKIT
- Antiquing

MATERIALS
- Earrings from Hands On p. 23

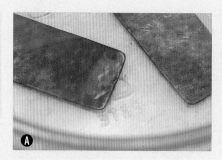

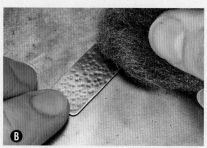

Clean the metal: If the metal has just been sanded, textured, and stamped, it is probably clean (oxidation-free). If not, scrub with superfine steel wool to remove any surface oxidation, wash in soapy water, and rinse.

Antique with liver of sulfur gel: Mix the solution in another bowl per the manufacturer's recommendations. It is usually as simple as adding a lump or few drops of gel to a few tablespoons of

warm water. Add the earrings **[A]**. Watch the color develop, remove the metal using tweezers, and rinse under cold running water. Continue the dipping and rinsing process until you like the look. Rinse thoroughly in running water.

Removing color on high surfaces: Allow the metal to air dry for a few minutes. Brush a piece of superfine steel wool

or fine-grit polishing paper across the surface to remove color from the high spots **[B]**. Be careful when using steel wool on shallow patterns; it can remove all the patina. ■

Your fabricated earrings are finished!

ETCHING

Etching allows you to create your own imagery on a metal surface. Sterling silver, fine silver, copper, nickel silver, and brass are etchable metals. I like to create my own freehand designs as in the Hands On exercise that follows. The beauty of this technique is that you need only the etching solution and fairly simple resist supplies such as permanent ink or nail polish, and you'll be able to create some fabulous designs on metal.

Etching tools & supplies

A rubber gloves

B plastic container with lid

C electrical tape

D needle tools

E plastic tweezers

F toothbrush

G brass-bristle brush

H toothpicks

I baking soda

J acetone

K ferric chloride etchant

YOU'LL ALSO NEED:
(not pictured)

• Ferric nitrate (to etch silver)

• Resists: permanent black markers, quick-dry nail polish, or solvent-based ink pad with rubber texture mats and roller

When metal with a resist applied is placed into etching solution, unprotected metal is slowly removed by a chemical reaction, resulting in a textured piece of metal. Wherever resist is applied, the surface will not be affected. Uncoated sections will be recessed areas with a subtly feathered texture.

I like to use low-tech options to create a resist design on metal: Draw freehand with permanent ink markers or colored nail polish, or stamp a design using a solvent-based inkpad such as Staz-On.

Etching copper, nickel silver, and brass: For these base metals, use **ferric chloride**. This chemical, used to etch copper circuit boards, is commonly sold as PCB Etchant Solution and is reusable, although the etching power will diminish with time. Use the solution full-strength from the bottle.

Sterling and fine-silver etching: To etch sterling or fine silver, use **ferric nitrate**, which is available from online chemical suppliers. Measure 300ml of distilled water into a plastic or glass (not metal) container. Measure 500 grams of ferric nitrate crystals, and slowly add them to the water in small (50 to 100-gram) increments. When the crystals dissolve, add the next increment. Stir the solution with a plastic or wood spoon. Remember what you learned in high school chemistry: "Don't add water to acids; always add the acids to the water." Store the solution in a thick-walled plastic bottle with a plastic (not metal) cap in a cool area.

⚠ **SAFETY Ferric chloride and ferric nitrate are corrosive poisons, so review the manufacturer's material safety data sheet, work in an area with good ventilation, use precaution when handling, and follow recommended disposal procedures. Use rubber gloves and safety glasses to avoid contact with eyes and skin. The solutions will stain, so wear an apron or old clothes and protect work surfaces.**

The etching process: As etching occurs, a superfine sediment is suspended in the mordant. Copper will etch reasonably well in 1–1½ hours, and nickel silver takes a bit longer at 1½–2 hours. Sterling silver takes at least 4 hours or so. It may take some trial and error to figure out how long to leave the metal in the etching solution. Check the depth of the etch every so often; if the etch is not deep enough, return the metal to the solution.

TIP Because fine silver and sterling silver require a longer time in the etchant, apply nail polish over the lines of the design to ensure the resist lasts through the etching process.

Size of etching samples: You can etch any size piece of metal as long as the plastic or glass container is large enough to contain the suspended piece with at least ¾" of mordant below it when it is suspended in the solution.

Thickness (gauge) of metal: You can etch any gauge of metal; base your choice of gauge on the end use of the etched metal. For example, to make a pair of pendant earrings, I'd use 24-gauge, and for bead caps, I would use 26-gauge.

hands on: ETCHING

This exercise is designed to encourage you to experiment with different types of resists on copper and nickel silver. This exercise is not part of the Hands On earrings project; you can make your etched pieces into small pendants, charms, or bead caps. I turned etched copper rectangles into charms and made the nickel silver disks into bead caps.

Prepare the metal pieces: Use a jeweler's saw to cut out some small geometric shapes from 24-gauge copper sheet and 26-gauge nickel silver sheet. You can use thinner metals, but you run the risk that the etching solution will eat through the metal. Wash the shapes in soapy water and dry them to remove oxidation and oils. File and smooth the edges and surfaces. Pay special attention to smoothing the surface you'll apply the design to; I use 400-grit polishing paper.

Marker-resist application: Use a fine-tip permanent marker to draw designs on the shapes **[A]**. Retrace the lines to ensure the design is solidly black; this is especially important if you don't add a nail polish overlay (described next). If your design

does not require fine detail, use a broad-tip marker. If you make a mistake, start over by removing the ink with alcohol or sandpaper. You can also use a pointed dental tool, a needle, or a T-pin to scrape away or adjust any stray marks. Use a broad-tip marker to cover the outer edge of the shapes completely **[B]**. This protects the edges from being etched. If desired, trace a border. If the disk or charm will be pierced, you'll drill the hole after etching.

Nail polish application: Applying an overlay of colored nail polish will result in a crisper etch. Place the shapes on an index card and pour a little puddle of nail polish on the card. Use a toothpick dipped in the polish to trace over the design. To avoid smudges, I hold the metal with one toothpick and use another to apply the nail polish **[C]**. You can spin the card around to reach all sides without having to risk touching wet polish. Use a T-pin or similar tool to scratch off any excess. Allow to dry.

Applying inked stamp designs: As an alternative, place a rubber texture mat face down on an inkpad and run a roller across the mat. Carefully position the

inked mat face down on the metal, and lightly roll across the mat **[D]**. Lift the mat without twisting it to avoid smudges. Use a marker to fill in sections of the ink resist that did not transfer well **[E]**. You can use rubber stamps in a similar way.

Back the metal with tape: Electrical tape works well for etching because it resists the etchant and it does not leave a sticky residue. Cut a piece of tape long enough to span the plastic dish plus few inches. Lay the tape on your work surface sticky side up. Fold over the ends of the tape. Center the shapes resist side up on the sticky side of the tape, allowing a few millimeters between each piece **[F]**. Turn over the tape with the shapes attached

TOOLKITS
• Etching, Cutting, Filing, Finishing, Drilling, Antiquing

MATERIALS
• 24-gauge copper and/or 26-gauge nickel silver sheet (3x10cm)
• Index card

A

B

C

D

E

and use your fingernail to adhere the shapes firmly on the tape [G].

Set up the etching: Carefully pour some of the etchant into the dish so the solution is 1" deep. Place the tape sticky side down across the top of the solution and over the edges of the dish or container, making sure the shapes are covered by the solution and there is at least ¾" of liquid below the metal. Secure the edges of the tape over the sides of the dish [H]. Cover the dish. For large pieces, position the metal so it is level in the solution. Pour more etchant into the dish if needed.

Check the progress: Check the pieces after 45–60 minutes for depth of etching (or after just 30–40 minutes if the solution is new). Wearing rubber gloves, carefully lift the tape and inspect the face of the metal. Drag a T-pin or toothpick across the face of the disk to check for the depth of the etching. If it is not deep enough, replace the metal in the solution for another 15–30 minutes and check again. Repeat until the etching has reached the desired depth.

If the level of liquid is too shallow (less than ½"), the buildup of metal sediment right below the etched surface may inhibit the etching process. Occasionally agitate the dish gently to disperse any sediment that develops and remove trapped air bubbles. As the etching proceeds, the solution will darken.

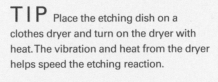

TIP Place the etching dish on a clothes dryer and turn on the dryer with heat. The vibration and heat from the dryer helps speed the etching reaction.

Cleanup: Use a funnel to pour the used solution into a storage container—it can be reused. As the solution ages, etching will take longer. Add fresh solution to speed the process. Do not pour the chemical down the drain.

Neutralize the metal: Pour 1–2 tablespoons of baking soda into a container and add water to make a paste. Remove the metal pieces from the tape, wipe off any residual etching solution with a paper towel, and use a toothbrush or cotton swab to rub the paste onto the metal [I]. Let it sit a few minutes. The baking soda neutralizes the etching process. You can rinse off the paste with running water and allow the rinse to go down the sink drain.

Remove the resist: Soak a portion of a paper towel with acetone and place the metal shapes face down on the towel for 10–15 seconds. Wipe off the nail polish and any remaining ink [J].

Cleanup: The metal pieces will be dull [K]. If you see ink or nail polish residue, you can use a piece of steel wool, a brass-bristle brush, or a 400-grit radial bristle disk to clean the surface.

Polish the metal edges: If there are some nicks in the edges of the metal from etching, use an extra-fine abrasive wheel to buff the edges smooth.

Antique and buff the pieces: Apply an antiquing solution to darken the metal. Use a 400-grit polishing stick to buff the high, flat surfaces. I rubbed a balled-up piece of 400-grit polishing paper across the recesses to remove some but not all of the dark color, revealing the background feathering pattern. If your etching is deeper, use a bristle disk wheel, a brass wheel, or superfine steel wool to bring back some metal highlights. ■

TUBE-RIVETING

Wire rivets and tube rivets are often called "cold connections" to distinguish them from "hot" metal connections made by soldering. In the exercise below, you'll set a large tube rivet in a stone.

Tube rivets are both pretty and practical in jewelry. They can connect multiple components, as in the Coral Clamshell necklace on p. 67, secure a bead cap on a bead, or be used as contrasting embellishment on a drilled stone.

Any diameter of tubing (even tiny crimp tubes) can be used to make a tube rivet, provided you have tools such as the center punches shown to flare the ends of the tube. For large tube rivets (about 4mm wide and larger), you'll flare the ends and then use a steel punch to flatten the ends into a smooth collar around the hole. For the projects in this book, get a range of center punches as shown. (Some metalsmiths use an eyelet-setting tool, sold for scrapbooking, for flaring the ends.) You'll need steel dapping punches (from your dapping set) with spherical ends from 5–14mm. Use a jeweler's saw and a bench pin or a tube cutter to cut the tubing to the length needed.

The rule of thumb for the length of tube needed for a rivet is the height of the item to be riveted plus the diameter of the tubing.

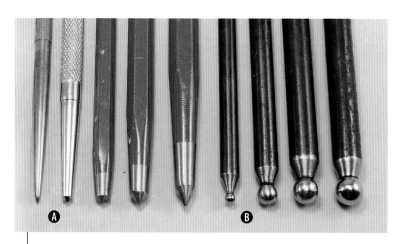

Tube-riveting tools

A graduated-size center punches

B graduated-size dapping punches

YOU'LL ALSO NEED:
(not pictured)

• Masking tape
• Tube cutter (optional)
• Toolkits: Torchwork, Filing, Forming & Forging, Finishing, Cutting

hands on: TUBE-RIVETING

TOOLKITS
• Tube-Riveting (plus kits listed above right)

MATERIALS
• Fine-silver tubing, 6.3mm outer diameter (2cm)
• River stone with 6.3mm diameter hole

TOOL NOTE

To flare this wide tubing, use center punches that are 6.3 and 6.8mm wide (measured at the base of the neck) and dapping punches in a progression of sizes from 7–14mm. Center punch sets can be purchased at most hardware stores.

This exercise details setting a 6mm wide fine-silver tube rivet into a river stone. Sterling silver and copper tubing also work well for tube rivets. You can use the resulting riveted stones in the bracelet project on p. 74.

Fit the tubing: The tubing must fit snugly into the hole in the stone. If there is too much of a gap between the inside of the hole and the tubing, the rivet will be hard to set and may bend as you try to set it.

Anneal the tubing: Annealing the tubing (either before or after it is cut to size) will allow you to work it more easily. Soft fine-silver tubing works well for setting tube rivets in fragile items such as lampwork

beads. This tubing is easier to forge than sterling silver tubing, but I still recommend annealing it. Heat the tubing until it reaches a soft, dull cherry red glow **[A]**. Quench and rinse.

Measure the tubing: Following the formula above, if my stone is 3mm tall and my tubing measures 6.3mm (outer

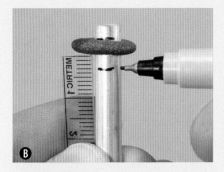

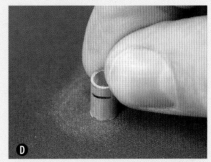

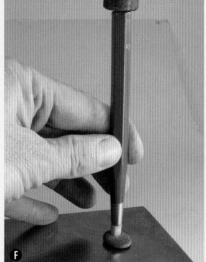

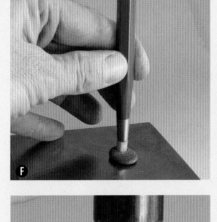

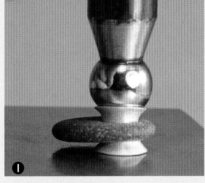

diameter), I'd cut a 9.3mm piece of tubing. For larger tube rivets, shorten the add-on measurement to about 80% of the tube diameter (in this example, I might cut a 8–8.5mm piece of tubing). This will make a slightly narrower collar on my rivet. Insert the tubing into the drilled stone, and mark the point where it should be cut [B]. I measured and marked about 3mm of metal tubing that will be rolled over to form a collar on each side of the stone. Remove the tubing from the stone. If the precut end is not perfectly flat, file it flat so it will create an even rivet collar.

Cut the tubing: Use a 3/0 saw blade to cut the tubing at the marked line [C]. If you do not have a tube cutter, place the tubing over the edge of a bench pin and saw at the marked line. The tubing may be difficult to hold, so work carefully to saw an even line. (If you do a lot of tube-riveting, you may want to buy a tube cutter.)

Sand and file the tube: The sawed end of the tube will be rough. Move the end in a circular motion on 320-grit silicon carbide sandpaper to remove the burr [D]. Smooth both ends and check to make sure all saw marks have been removed. Use a round needle file to remove any burrs on the inside edge of the tube [E].

Set the rivet: Use a 6.3mm center punch followed by a 6.8mm wide center punch to flare the tube ends. Place the sanded tube into the stone and place it on a bench block. With the tip of the center punch in the top of the tube, lightly tap the top of

the punch with a utility hammer several times [F]. The end should flare slightly. Flare the opposite end in the same way. Switch to a slightly larger center punch and repeat until the tube ends are flared equally and they are wide enough to hold the tube in the hole [G].

Form the rivet collar: Use a series of steel dapping punches from about 7–14mm wide to fold over the edges of the tube. Make sure the stone is centered between the ends of the tube before you start. Place the smallest dapping punch on the top of the tube and strike lightly with a utility

hammer a few times. Make sure the punch and hammer strike is straight down [H]. Flip the assembly over and repeat. Work back and forth, flipping from top to bottom, always hammering lightly. You might need four or five graduated sizes of punches to fold the collar over [I]. Work slowly and gently to avoid cracking the stone. Place the end of one of the larger dapping punches on the collar and hammer the punch, working around the high edge of the collar to fold it over [J].

Use the wide, slightly domed face of a chasing hammer to fold the outer edge

of the collar down toward the stone **[K]**. Place the assembly at the edge of a bench block. (I do this step at eye level so I can see the collar curve down.) Using light, soft, brushing strokes, work around each end, brushing the edge of the lip with the hammer so the edge curves down and contacts the stone.

Polish the rivet surface: Use an extra-fine grit abrasive bullet to buff the neck and inner edge of the rivet **[L]** and an extra-

fine wheel to buff the surface and outer edge **[M]**. Use 400-grit polishing paper to buff each rivet to a uniform, satin finish. ■

TIP If you're riveting an item that's easily scratched or nicked, such as glass or metal, place small pieces of thin masking tape on the surfaces to protect it from nicks as you form the rivet collar.

These rivets are about 1cm wide with a 5–6mm inner diameter. The stones are about 1.5x2cm.

hands on: MAKING JUMP RINGS

TOOLKITS
• Cutting
• Torchwork

MATERIALS
• 18-gauge square sterling silver wire (30–40cm)

I often buy small jump rings ready to use, but I always make my own large rings. These rings are made from square wire, which tends to twist as you form a coil. Work slowly to keep the orientation of the wire constant.

TIP This Hands On exercise is not part of the rectangular earrings project, but the jump rings you make can be used in many types of jewelry projects.

Anneal the wire: This heavy square wire needs to be annealed (see p. 35) so you'll be able to wrap it around the mandrel. (Fine-silver wire and lighter gauges of sterling silver may be soft enough to work without annealing; the resulting rings will be stiff, which is ideal.)

Wind the wire around a mandrel: If the wire was coiled for annealing, open the coil and straighten the wire. Remove any twists from the square wire so that it lies flat. (If you are using round wire, this is not an issue.) You can use any type of thin cylinder as a mandrel (a wood dowel or a pen, for example) to make the jump rings. Wrap the wire around the form 5–10 times. Keep the square wire flat against the dowel so it does not twist as it is wrapped around the form **[A]**. If it starts to twist, use chainnose or flatnose pliers to reorient it flat **[B]**.

Saw the jump rings: Mark a straight line across the top of the coil with a permanent marker. Tighten the top of a

3/0 saw blade into the saw frame, thread the coil on the blade, and tighten the base of the blade. You can clamp the back of the saw frame in a bench vise or balance it against a table edge. If braced against a table edge, do not push into the saw frame; this will loosen the tension.

Pinch the coil tightly at the top and bottom, and align the mark on the coil with the blade **[C]**. Apply downward pressure and slowly move the coil back and forth, keeping the mark aligned with the blade until a groove is cut in all rings. The cutting action occurs on the "away" stroke. Focus pressure on the farthest ring, because this ring will cut first. The rings will fall off one by one. ■

TORCHWORK
tools & techniques

Mention the word "torch" and it often sends a chill down the backs of new students. My response to that reaction is if you can cook on a gas stove or grill, you can handle a torch—and it can actually be fun. A project as simple as making headpins is a bit magical: Watching the wire end bead up into a shiny silver ball in the flame is fun for first timers.

Torch techniques

I did not take to soldering automatically and, because of my fears, I designed most of my early jewelry projects to avoid the need for it. But eventually I decided to embrace and practice the technique, which allowed me to create more intricate designs. You might be surprised to know that the hardest part about soldering is not the step that uses the torch—it is the preparation required to ensure a successful solder join.

This section presents a sampling of basic techniques that require a torch. The handiest of them is making your own balled headpins out of wire. You'll also learn how to anneal metal to make it more workable and the basic chip soldering technique used to join two pieces of metal. You'll also find a "Hands On" exercise that teaches you how to make the soldered variation of the earrings introduced on p. 7.

Torch systems

All of the projects in this book can be completed using a butane torch sold for jewelry making. These simple-to-use, refillable torches are great for a beginner to learn with, and they may be all you need for small-scale jewelry projects.

Two sizes of butane torches are commonly sold for jewelry making: the standard size, often called a micro torch (left), and a torch capable of a larger flame, the jumbo torch (right).

You'll see two sizes of butane torches on the market: the standard size, often called a micro torch, and a torch capable of a larger flame (the jumbo torch). These torches are available from online retailers and some hardware stores. I don't recommend using a small torch designed for cooking (often referred to as a crème brûlée torch). I use an industrial-grade butane torch with an electronic ignition and a flame size adjuster.

A disadvantage of the micro torch is that the flame isn't big enough for certain large projects. Conversely, jumbo butane torches—even those with a flame adjuster—may have too big of a flame for small projects unless you are skilled at handling it. You may want to begin with a micro torch and add a jumbo torch if you are doing a lot of torchwork. Handheld butane torches require a small canister of filtered butane gas. A butane flame burns at about 2500°F/1371°C.

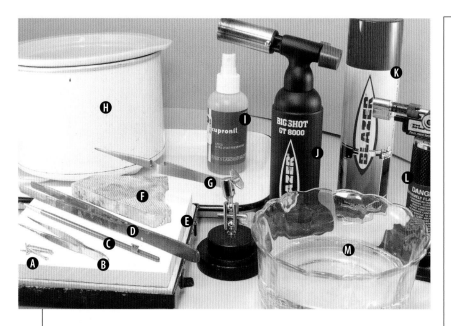

Torchwork tools

A cotter pins

B tweezers

C fine-tip paintbrush

D copper tongs

E ceramic Solderite boards on spin table

F honeycomb solder board

G third hand with crosslocking tweezers

H pickle pot

I spray flux

J jumbo butane torch

K butane gas refill

L micro butane torch

M quench bowl

As the flame weakens, you'll know it's time to refill your torch: With the torch upside down, press and hold the fuel nozzle on the filling nipple.

Filling a butane torch: Move to a location away from open flames or other torches in use. Turn the torch upside down, exposing the filling nipple. Hold the torch at arm's length and turn the torch nozzle away from your body. Place the fuel canister nozzle on the filling nipple. Compress the fuel nozzle down onto the torch. You should hear gas entering the torch. The torch might take 10–20 seconds to fill, depending on its size. When the torch is full, the gas will sputter out from the fuel nozzle. Turn the torch over and allow the gas to settle for a minute or two before lighting.

Other torch systems: As you progress in jewelry making, you may want to explore the difference between these small, refillable torches and a larger, more-powerful (and more expensive) torch such as an acetylene/air setup or a mixed-gas unit. My suggestion is to take classes at your local technical college or art school and test the soldering equipment there. If you decide to move to a larger torch, check your local fire regulations and consult your renters or homeowners insurance policy.

A few common systems used by jewelers include an acetylene/air setup and a mixed gas setup such as oxygen/acetylene or oxygen/propane. A mixed-gas unit popular with jewelry makers is the Little Torch system, which is sold as an all-in-one unit with small compressed tanks on a portable caddy system. Each setup has advantages and disadvantages—consider factors such as cost, size of flame, size of equipment, and transportability.

Torch work station

Work surfaces: You will need a heatproof and flameproof board designed for annealing and soldering, and you'll have a variety of choices. I use a **Solderite board** (6x6" or 12x12"), and I often place the board on top of a metal spin table designed for soldering that rotates 360 degrees so you can get at the work from all sides. This solder board is highly heat reflective, allowing the torch heat to reflect back to the metal and keep it hot.

A **charcoal soldering block** is also highly heat reflective and creates a reducing

FLAME TYPES

An **adjustable-flame torch** allows you to control the amount of oxygen being burned. With a little practice, you can learn to adjust the flame type to suit the project you are working on. More oxygen being burned creates a hot flame and less oxygen creates a cool flame. To keep things simple at the start, set your torch to a neutral flame.

All three flames contain a bright blue inner cone surrounded by a darker, cobalt blue border flame. The hottest portion of these flames is at the tip of the bright blue inner cone. Look closely at the shape of this bright blue cone to determine whether it is oxidizing, neutral, or reducing.

Oxidizing flame: This flame has a loud air flow. It is hot and oxygen-rich. The bright blue inner cone has a sharp, pointed tip. Some nonadjustable butane torches will produce only this type of flame. This flame heats metal quickly and is good for balling wire ends, but use it with care—it can produce unwanted firescale.

Neutral flame: This flame has a balanced mixture of oxygen and gas. The tip of the bright blue inner cone is softly pointed compared with an oxidizing flame. The neutral flame is good for most soldering projects.

Reducing flame: This flame is gas-rich and burns less oxygen than the other two flame types. The tip of the bright blue inner cone is bushy and larger than the other two flame types. This flame is the coolest of the three flame types. It is ideal for annealing metal, but does not work well for some soldering projects.

Clockwise from left: Solderite board on a spin table, charcoal block, and a honeycomb ceramic block.

atmosphere, which helps reduce the oxidation that forms as you heat metal.

A **honeycomb ceramic block** has pin-sized holes, allowing heat to dissipate quickly, which is helpful when working with large metal pieces. I often use small pieces of honeycomb ceramic blocks as a support structure when soldering complicated 3-dimensional metal pieces. Ceramic firebricks that are used in pottery kilns can also be used as a soldering surface.

When you use a torch only for balling wire ends, any type of flameproof surface such as a large ceramic tile will be sufficient as a work surface. Never point the flame directly at the tile.

My work station: I use a metal lab table as my primary soldering bench. I lined the surface of the table with concrete landscape pavers; my solder board sits on the pavers. Over my bench, a cooktop hood vents to the outside through a dryer vent flap. My acetylene torch tank with regulators is chained to the legs of the table. A mini crockpot filled with pickle sits at the back corner of my bench.

When I use my butane torch at other workbenches, I protect the tabletops with a 12x12" heatproof ceramic board or piece of galvanized sheet metal, and place my soldering surface on top.

A freestanding lab table is my main soldering station.

BALLING WIRE ENDS

If you're new to working with a torch, try this easy technique to help you get a feel for using the tool. A butane torch that offers hands-free operation is ideal. Any gauge of wire will ball up, but heavy-gauge wires will require the hot flame of a jumbo butane torch.

Fine-silver wire will ball up beautifully with a clean, shiny, and round ball at the end. Sterling silver wire will also ball up, but the end will be pitted, blackened (heavily oxidized), and often oblong. To help prevent oxidation, dip the wire end in some soldering paste or liquid flux before heating. You can use some fine and extra-fine abrasive polishing wheels to buff the ends into a uniform shape and finish. A dip in a pickle bath will clean the end. You can ball the ends of copper wire as well; use a hot jumbo butane torch.

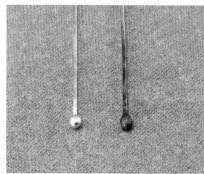

Fine-silver balled wire (left) and sterling silver wire (right).

🔴 **SAFETY Wear safety glasses when working with flames and molten wire.**

hands on: BALLING WIRE ENDS

TOOLKIT
• Torchwork

MATERIALS
• 18- or 20-gauge fine-silver wire (20cm)

This pair of balled-end wires can be used as earring wires.

Set up the torch: Place the torch on a heatproof surface pointing away from you and anything flammable such as paper or curtains. Keep your free hand away from the flame in case the ball melts off the wire.

Prepare and ball up the wire: Cut the wire into two 10cm sections. Hold a wire vertically with the tweezers. Heat the tweezers tip for a few seconds, holding the wire perpendicular to the flame **[A]**. Place the end of the wire just beyond the tip of the bright-blue inner cone **[B]**. In a few seconds, the flame will start to turn orange and the end of the wire will start to ball **[C]**. The ball will enlarge, turn molten **[D]**, and continue to melt, moving up the wire **[E]**. When the ball is the size you want, remove the wire from the flame and hold it without moving until the ball and wire tip turn silver. Quench. If the ball is not large enough, reheat it until it is the correct size. If you continue to heat the wire, the ball will eventually fall off. (A second dish of water can be placed below the flame to catch any balls that might fall off.) Ball the end of the other wire in the same way. Straighten the wires by rolling them between two bench blocks. ■

A

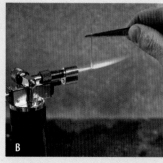

B

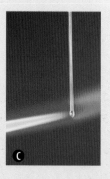

C

D

E

ANNEALING

As you work with a piece of metal, it often becomes work-hardened and difficult to manipulate. Annealing metal is not always necessary, but it can help make pieces more receptive to soldering or make jobs such as using a disk cutter or doming metal easier.

Annealing provides forming flexibility. During annealing, metal is heated to a temperature that allows its crystalline structure to relax and soften.

To anneal sterling silver, fine silver, nickel, or copper, heat to a dull red color. (You'll be able to see the color best under dim lighting.) A jumbo butane torch will allow you to anneal large pieces of metal (4x4" or larger). A micro butane torch will work to anneal small pieces of sheet and wire.

Flux protects metal from the oxidation that occurs during heating and acts as a temperature indicator that is helpful for annealing silver; it turns from dry, powdery white to clear at 1100°F, which is the temperature that silver alloys need to reach to be annealed.

hands on: ANNEALING

TOOLKIT
• Torchwork

MATERIALS
• Copper sheet of any gauge and size
• Fine-silver, sterling silver, or copper wire

Apply flux: Dim the room lights to help you see the color of the metal as it is heated. Place the metal on a solder board or charcoal block. Place the board or charcoal on a secondary heatproof surface such as a landscape paver or a sheet of galvanized aluminum. Apply a light coat of spray or paste flux. Paste flux is a bit more durable with heat and provides better firescale protection than spray flux.

I annealed copper in this example. Although you don't need flux to prevent oxidation when annealing copper, it will help you know when the metal reaches the correct temperature.

Heat the metal: Heat lightly with a torch. As the flux dries, it will turn powdery white **[A]**. If you are using spray flux, apply more while you continue heating until the whole surface is evenly coated. Flip the metal and repeat the fluxing and heating process. It does not matter which surface of the metal is facing up during annealing. Apply direct heat to the metal. The powdery white flux will turn clear and transparent **[B]**. Move the torch in circles over the metal surface. When the metal reaches the correct annealing color (cherry-red in the case of copper), keep the torch moving over the surface for approximately one minute **[C]**. Don't allow the metal to get hotter (bright orange).

Pick up the metal with a heavy-duty tweezers and carefully quench it in a dish of cool water. Place the metal in a heated pickle bath for a few minutes to remove any surface oxidation. Remove any residual oxidation using 220- or 320-grit sandpaper.

To anneal wire: Wrap wire into a coil and heat and flux in a similar manner. Keep the flame tip fairly close to the wire while moving the torch flame in quick circles around the wire. As the wire heats, the flux will turn clear **[D]**. Continue the circular heating motion. Watch for a pale, dull purplish/red color, which indicates it is at the annealing temperature. Continue heating for approximately one minute. Pick up the coil with metal tweezers. The wire will be very hot at this point. Quench, pickle, rinse, and dry. ■

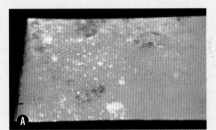

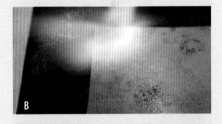

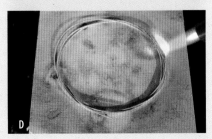

hands on: SOLDERING

Here's a variation of the fabricated earrings we built in the previous exercises. In this project, you'll start with similar components and then solder a curved piece of sterling silver square wire to the base rectangles.

TOOLKIT
• Torchwork

MATERIALS
• 2 18-gauge sterling silver rectangles (14x30mm)
• 18-gauge sterling silver square wire (12cm)

The tips of the wire extend just beyond the edge of the metal base in this earring design.

Prepare the base pieces: Prepare the base rectangles in the same way as before: Smooth the edges and corners, texture them as desired, and drill holes at the top. Do not antique the rectangles before soldering. If the rectangles cup slightly during texturing, flatten them on a bench block with a rawhide mallet.

Prepare the wire: Cut the wire in half and straighten each piece with chainnose pliers. The square wire will be fairly stiff. Use a round form or a pair of pliers to curve the wire as shown **[A]**.

Check the fit: Place each wire on a base and check the fit: You should not see any gaps between them **[B]**. If you see a gap, flatten the wire by placing it on a bench block and striking it firmly with the rawhide mallet. Or, place the wire between two blocks and strike the top block with the mallet.

Anneal: If you still see a gap after straightening the wire, you may need to anneal the base or the wire to relax the metal structure and allow it to be flattened with the rawhide mallet.

Clean the metal: Sand the side of the wire and base that will be soldered with 320- or 400-grit sandpaper. A quick rinse with water and a brief soak in pickle afterward will help ensure that the metal is extra-clean.

Prepare the solder: You can use any type of solder (hard, medium, easy, or extra easy) for this single-join project. Follow the solder preparation instructions on p. 36 to prepare pallions for this project.

Flux application and project setup: Place a base front side up on a solder board or charcoal block. Apply heat for several seconds using the outer tip of the flame of a micro butane torch (or a jumbo butane torch set to the lowest flame size). Spray the metal surface lightly with liquid flux. The flux will adhere more evenly if the metal is preheated, but do not heat the

metal longer than for a few seconds to avoid oxidation.

Heat the metal until the flux dries powdery white. Repeat the flux application and heating process until the area that will be soldered is covered with flux. The metal on the left shows flux applied in a uniform transparent film and the metal on the right shows flux too thick and patchy **[C]**. The back does not need to be coated with flux. Any oxidation that occurs on the back during soldering will clear off in the pickle bath.

Place the curved silver wire on the base. Dip a fine-tip paintbrush in the flux solution, dab off any excess, and touch the tip of the brush to a solder pallion to pick it up.

Place a pallion near the top of the square wire. Each pallion must touch both the wire and the base. Evenly space five or six solder pallions along the wire, between the wire and the base **[D]**. A spin table under your solder board allows you to check solder position from all sides

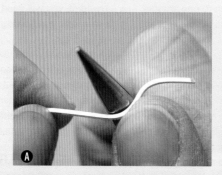

A

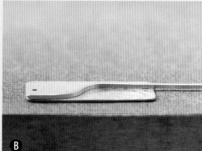

B

C

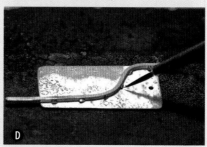

D

without disturbing the placement. Place the assembly so the solder on the side of the square wire is farthest away from you.

Preheat the work surface: Remember that solder flows towards heat. Slowly start to heat the project from above. Don't heat the metal too fast or the flux may boil up and pop the pallions out of place. (If this happens, use a solder pick to reposition them.) Make a wide circular motion around the project with the tip of the dark blue outer flame touching the charcoal block **[E]**. Don't touch the metal with the flame at this point. Enough heat will transfer to heat the metal and start to dry any remaining flux. The dried flux around each pallion acts as a temporary glue.

Focus the torch flame on the metal sheet: After 10–15 seconds, bring the flame tip closer to the base metal sheet, but still avoid any direct contact with the wire and solder **[F]**. Continue the circular torch movement over the metal. You can still see the solder pallions at this point.

Flux turns clear: As you continue to heat the metal, the powdery, white flux will start to turn clear and transparent—the sign that the solder pallions are about to melt and flow. When the flux turns clear, quickly move the torch to the bottom of the project (nearest you) and orient the flame tip low and horizontal to the soldering block. Point the flame toward the wire with the tip of the bright blue inner cone close to the metal sheet. Run the flame tip back and forth, parallel to the wire.

As the metal gets hotter, the surface will start to take on a sweaty/shimmery look **[G]**. The solder usually flows at this point. (Note that the pallions are no longer visible in this photo.) Continue to heat for just a few more seconds as the metal turns a low, dull gray-orange **[H]**. Quickly remove the torch, allow the metal to cool

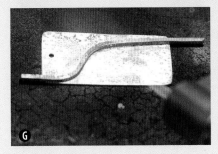
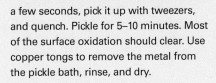

a few seconds, pick it up with tweezers, and quench. Pickle for 5–10 minutes. Most of the surface oxidation should clear. Use copper tongs to remove the metal from the pickle bath, rinse, and dry.

Cleanup: If any solder pooled or did not flow well, clean it up with an extra-fine-grit abrasive knife-edge disk or wheel **[I]**. Hold the wheel at the base of the square wire. Use a 400-grit radial bristle disk to remove any excess surface oxidation **[J]**.

Finish the square wires: Trim the tip of each wire end, leaving about 1mm extending over the edge of the base. Use a needle file or an abrasive wheel to round off each tip. You can also use a standard shaped wheel to buff the surface of the square to wire to a uniform polish.

Complete and assemble the project: Complete the earrings as described in the Fabrication section. ∎

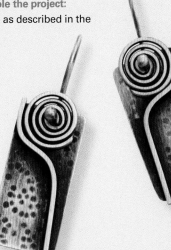

PROJECTS

SWEET & EASY PEARL DROP
earrings

Make simple and elegant earrings from a pair of pearls on hand-forged fine-silver earring wires. You'll learn how to drill pearl holes larger to fit onto handmade earring wires.

TOOLKITS
- Cutting
- Torchwork
- Drilling
- Forming & Forging
- Filing
- Finishing

ADDITIONAL TOOLS & SUPPLIES
- Diamond drill bits: tapered and various cylinders (1mm, 1.5mm)
- Small dish of water

MATERIALS
- 20-gauge fine-silver wire (14–16cm)

BEADS
- 2 drilled pearls, 12mm

Finished length: 2.5cm

Prepare the earring wires

Cut the wire into two 7cm pieces. Use a torch to create a 2–2.5mm balled end on each wire (see Balling wire ends, p. 34) **[A]**. Quench, rinse, and dry the wires.

For each wire: Place a wire between two metal bench blocks. Slide the top block back and forth for a few seconds, rolling the wire between the blocks to straighten it **[B]**.

Enlarge the pearl holes

Check the fit of the pearls on the 20-gauge wire; you may need to drill them larger.

🚫 SAFETY Use a GFCI outlet with the rotary tool for drilling underwater. Hold the pearl by its sides while drilling to prevent puncturing your finger.

For each pearl: Wet the pearl with water and use a tapered diamond drill bit to drill one end for 2–3 seconds **[C]**. Rinse the pearl. Repeat on the other side. Don't try to penetrate the hole from end to end with this bit; just flare both ends slightly.

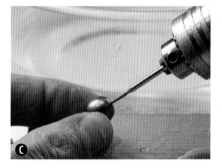

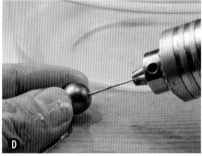

Dip the pearl in water. Use a 1mm diamond-coated cylinder bit to slowly drill the hole. Push gently against the pearl, lightly pulsing the bit while drilling for 2–5 seconds **[D]**.

Dip the pearl in water, drill again for 2–5 seconds, and dip in water. Make sure your fingers are always clear of the lower hole. Wipe the end of the bit off to clean it. Repeat this process from both ends of the pearl until the bit has completely pierced the pearl **[E]**.

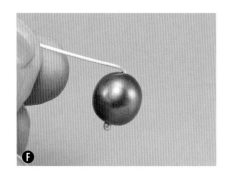

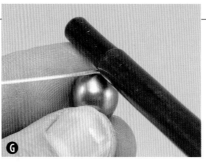

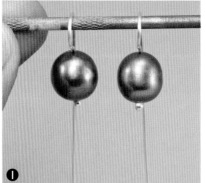

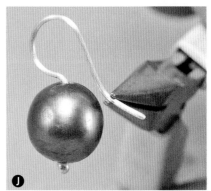

Use a 1.4–1.5mm diamond drill bit and alternate 2–3 seconds of drilling with a water rinse to further enlarge the hole. Flush the pearl with water to clean it of all pearl dust.

Shape the earring wires

For each wire: Smooth any burrs on the wire end that might keep it from easily entering the hole, and test whether the pearl can slide easily onto the wire. String the pearl on the wire and, holding the pearl, bend the wire forward in a 90-degree angle directly over the pearl **[F]**.

Using a straight ballpoint pen or a wood dowel as a mandrel, form the earring wire. Place the mandrel over the pearl at the bend in the wire **[G]**. Push the wire up and tightly around the mandrel to create the earring curve **[H]**.

Check the length

Hang the earrings on a file handle to see if the pearls hang at the same point **[I]**. Don't worry about the length of the wire tails at this point. If one earring body is slightly longer than the other, place the mandrel in the curve near the pearl and pull some of the slack out behind the curve. Recheck the length of the earrings.

Trim the earring wires to the same length behind the pearls. Use flatnose or chainnose pliers to bend each wire at the

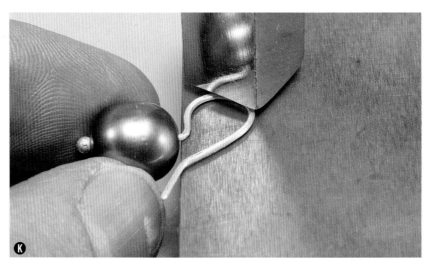

same point at the back of each pearl as shown to help hold the earring in place against the earlobe **[J]**.

Forge the earring wires

For each earring: Place the earring wire on a metal bench block with the pearl hanging off the edge. Use a smooth faced riveting or chasing hammer to lightly forge the wire **[K]**. Be careful to avoid striking the pearl.

Round and soften the end of each earring wire with the flat face of a needle file, polishing paper, or a cup bur. Being careful to avoid the pearls, use a 400-grit polishing stick to buff out any nicks in the wire surface **[L]**. Use chainnose pliers to straighten any bends in the wires. Wash the earrings in soapy water, rinse, and dry. ■

SILVER BAR & RUBY *earrings*

This earrings project is a good introduction to forging wire as you work with a planishing hammer to forge thick-gauge round wire flat. You can use a chasing hammer, but the heavy weight of the planishing hammer will broaden the metal faster.

TOOLKITS
- Cutting
- Forming & Forging
- Drilling
- Filing
- Finishing

MATERIALS
- 14-gauge fine-silver or sterling silver wire (9cm)
- 2 24-gauge sterling silver eyepins

BEADS
- 2 faceted ruby beads, 5x8mm

Prepare the wire
Flush-cut two 4.5cm pieces of 14-gauge fine-silver wire. Use a hand file to smooth and flatten the ends of each piece. Straighten each wire by rolling it between two metal bench blocks.

Forge and smooth the wire
For each wire: Place the wire on a metal bench block perpendicular to the front of the block. The hammer action for forging is more of a brushing stroke rather than an up-and-down strike. Hold the top of the wire on the block and strike the wire with the middle of the curved hammer face. Keep the face flat so the edges do not nick the wire and avoid striking the bench block.

Finished length: 6cm

DESIGN NOTE

An eyepin is a straight, hardened wire with a round loop at one end. Use the thickest gauge eyepin that fits the hole of your beads. Eyepins are hardened by the manufacturer, and the hardness may vary from half-hard to three-quarters hard. Despite being extremely thin, they make a durable earring wire.

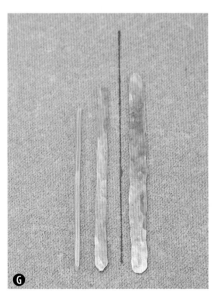

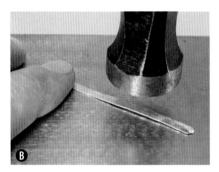

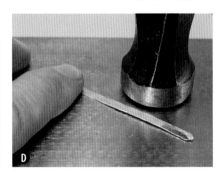

Finish each hammer stroke by sweeping the hammer down along the wire length [A]. Continue forging the length of the wire to the end. Flip the wire over and repeat. Turn the wire to repeat the forging process on the top end until the wire is about 2mm wide.

Place the wire diagonally on the bench block with the hammer face flat so the edges do not nick the wire [B]. (The photos show the action for right-handers.) Visualize striking the wire on its right side [C]. Finish each hammer stroke

by sweeping the hammer across the wire, out, and up [D]. As you bring the hammer down on the metal, finish with an upward, brush-like stroke. Think of it like the motion of brushing crumbs off a table. Forge down the length of the wire. Flip the wire over and repeat on the other side. The wire may curve because of the forging [E].

Flip the wire over and forge the right side again with sideways strokes. This should broaden the wire and even out the curvature [F]. (Use a metal ruler or draw a

straight line for reference.) Work back and forth from top to bottom until the wire is 4–5mm wide. The metal will be curvy and uneven. The bar on the right is about 6cm long; it gained 1.5cm through forging [G].

Use wire cutters to trim from the top and bottom of the bar so it measures 4.5cm. Smooth the ends with a needle file. Use an extra-fine abrasive wheel to smooth the corners [H] and any uneven spots along each edge. Bevel the edges on the front and back.

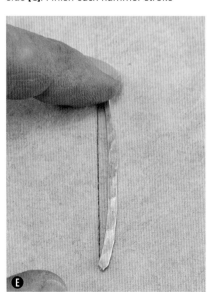

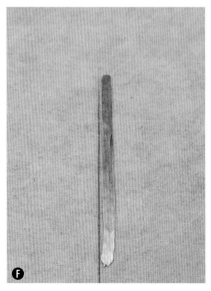

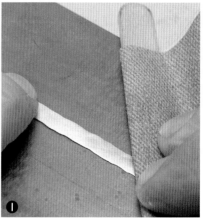

Pierce and finish the bars

For each bar: Mark a centered spot for drilling about 1mm from the top of each bar. Make a dimple with a center punch and drill a hole with a #60 drill bit from front to back. Remove the burr at the back of each hole with sandpaper.

Sand both sides of each bar with either the 400-grit sandpaper or polishing paper. To remove stubborn scratches, use a coarser grit of sandpaper and finish with a fine-grit polishing stick **[I]**. Sand in one direction across the metal, turn the sandpaper 180 degrees, and sand again.

String the beads and form the earring wires

For each earring: Holding the eyepin loop with two pairs of chainnose pliers, bring one pair toward you to slightly open the loop. String the metal bar on the loop and close the loop. String a bead onto the eyepin above the bar. Bend the wire over the bead toward the front of the bar **[J]**. Using a pen or other mandrel, bend the wire back and around to form the earring wire **[K]**.

Finish the earring wires

Check whether the earring wires match in shape and adjust if necessary. Forge them lightly with a riveting or chasing hammer to flatten and harden the wires slightly **[L]**.

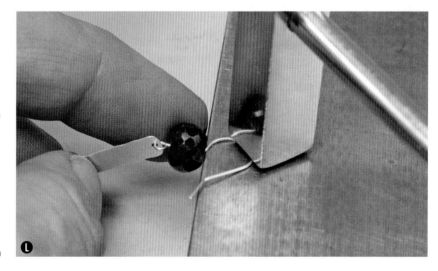

Remove any nicks in the earring wires using a 400-grit polishing stick. Trim the ends to the same length, make a small bend in each end, and smooth the wire ends. Wash the earrings in soapy water, rinse, and dry. ■

KIMONO *earrings*

This project is a good introduction to sawing metal shapes, and the design is an attractive display for a favorite pair of square or rectangular beads that are fairly flat. Tourmaline comes in a variety of colors, so I took advantage of the variation and chose beads that didn't match. This earring design also lends itself well to beads that are semitransparent.

TOOLKITS
- Cutting
- Filing
- Drilling
- Forming & Forging
- Finishing
- Antiquing
- Torchwork

ADDITIONAL SUPPLIES
- Cardstock or plastic grid sheet for template

MATERIALS
- 26-gauge sterling silver sheet (2.5x5cm)
- 20-gauge fine-silver wire for earring wires (22–26cm)
- 20- to 24-gauge fine-silver wire for bead wire (5–6cm)

BEADS
- 2 rectangular beads, about 13x16mm

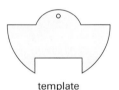

template

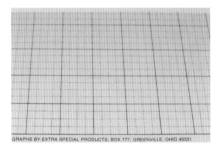

GRAPHS BY EXTRA SPECIAL PRODUCTS, BOX 777, GREENVILLE, OHIO 45331

You can find this plastic sheet at a hobby or sewing store. Use it to make solid, reusable templates.

Make the template
Trace the template onto light cardstock or a piece of gridded plastic sheet and cut it out.

Saw out the pattern
Use an ultra-fine-tip marker to trace the template twice onto a piece of 26-gauge sterling silver sheet. Using a 6/0 or 7/0 blade, saw out the two shapes, sawing slightly outside the tracing lines. You can use a pair of fine shears to cut out the pattern, but it will be difficult to cut out the lower square section without distorting the metal.

Sand the cutouts
Sand both sides of the pieces on 320-grit silicon carbide sandpaper to remove the sawing burrs. If there are any uneven sanding spots, use a rawhide mallet to flatten the pieces and sand again.

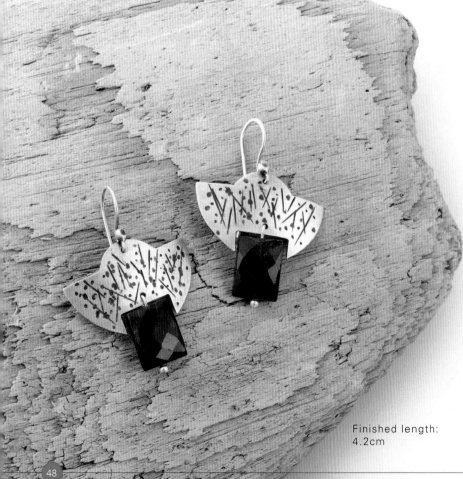

Finished length: 4.2cm

File the edges and corners

Use a coarse, flat hand file to file off any major imperfections on each metal piece. For the lower cutout section, use a flat needle file to square off the three straight edges **[A]**. The two pieces will most likely not be the same shape or size at this point. To make them match, place the smaller piece on top of the larger one. Line up as much of the outer edges as possible. Use a fine-tip marker to trace onto the exposed excess of the lower piece. Working at the edge of a bench pin, use a coarse file to remove the excess metal **[B]**. Sand to remove any burrs. Repeat this process until the two pieces match. Use a file to round the four points of each piece.

Bevel the edges and polish

Use an extra-fine abrasive wheel to remove any sawing marks from the edge of each piece **[C]**. Bevel the top edge of each piece for a nice finishing touch **[D]**. Repeat on the back. Alternatively, you can also polish and bevel by hand with a polishing stick. When finished, sand both sides with 400-grit polishing paper until the surfaces are uniformly smooth.

Drill two holes in each piece

Use an ultra-fine-tip marker to mark the drilling holes (as shown on the template) for the earring wires. Use a center punch to create a dimple at each mark, and drill each hole with a #60 high-speed twist drill bit. Sand off the metal burr that forms at the back of each hole. Check the fit of each hole with 20-gauge wire. If the hole is too small, enlarge it by twisting a round needle file in it.

Stamp/texture the pieces

I used several tools to create texture: the peen end of a chasing hammer **[E]**, two sizes of line stamps, and two dull center punches **[F]**. Use a utility hammer and metal bench block with the steel stamps. The texturing tools will make the metal dome upward. To flatten it, flip it over and strike it with a rawhide mallet.

Antique the textured metal

Antique the metal with liver of sulfur. Use a piece of superfine steel wool or a 400-grit polishing stick to remove some of the patina as desired.

Dome each metal piece

Place each piece face down in a shallow depression of a wood dapping block and use the wood dapping punch and a hammer to push the piece into the depression **[G]**. Make sure to dome out to the very edges of the metal.

Ball the earring wire

Cut the 20-gauge wire into two equal pieces. Use a torch to ball one end of each wire. Place each balled end on a metal bench block and strike it lightly with a chasing hammer to create two flattened faces. Roll each wire between two metal bench blocks to straighten and work-harden the wires. If desired, antique and buff the wires.

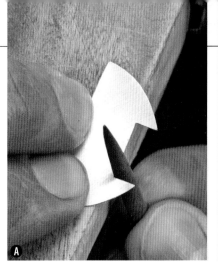

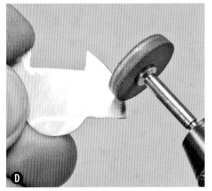

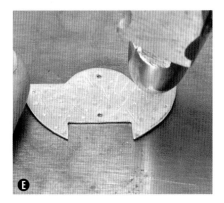

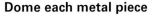

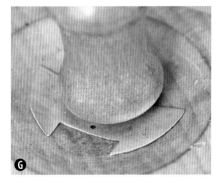

DESIGN NOTE

The thinnest wire I use to make earring wires is 24-gauge. If your bead holes are too small to fit 24-gauge wire, use manufactured headpins, which are already hardened and will hold a shape.

Form the earring wire

For each earring wire: String a balled earring wire through the upper hole in the metal piece. Orient one flattened face of the balled wire end as shown, and curve the wire around the outside of the chainnose pliers jaw next to the balled end **[H]**. Lower the metal piece down into the wire curve. Use chainnose pliers to pinch the balled end over the top of the metal piece until it touches the curved wire. Bend the wire forward over the front of the metal piece and wrap it back over a narrow mandrel **[I]**. Use a riveting hammer followed by chasing hammer to lightly forge the earring wires to add stiffness. Round off the wire ends and sand off any hammer nicks.

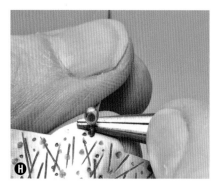

Make the bead wire

Choose the thickest gauge of fine-silver wire that will fit through the beads. The hole in my beads was large enough for 22-gauge wire. Ball both ends and cut the wire in half. Antique the wires if desired.

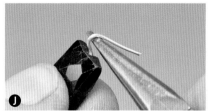

For each earring: String a wire through the base of a bead. Use chainnose pliers to bend the wire over the front of the bead. Make a tight curve by wrapping the wire over the outside of the pliers jaw **[J]**. String the wire through the lower hole of a metal piece. At the back of the metal piece, trim the wire to ¼". Smooth the wire end if desired. Use pliers to fold the wire end down into a loop **[K]**. Wash the earrings with soapy water, rinse, and dry. ■

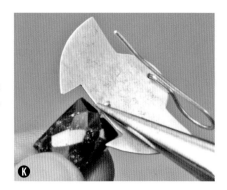

variations

These earrings feature green tourmaline beads on flat, nontextured metal. Small spirals made with 20-gauge wire add interest. The balled wire end is held in place with a crimp bead.

These beads are made of old Roman glass. I used texturing hammers instead of stamps and domed the metal, but not quite as deeply as in the lead project.

This pair uses colorful, square agate beads. The metal was textured with hammers and slightly domed.

WRIST CANDY
bracelet

TOOLKITS
- Cutting
- Filing
- Finishing
- Drilling
- Antiquing
- Forming & Forging
- Torchwork

ADDITIONAL TOOLS & SUPPLIES
- Cardstock or plastic grid sheet for template
- Crimping pliers (optional)
- Rotary tumbler with stainless steel shot and burnishing fluid (optional)

MATERIALS
- 16-gauge sterling silver wire (7.5cm)
- 16-gauge fine-silver wire (16cm)
- 24-gauge fine-silver wire (28cm)
- 20-gauge sterling or fine-silver wire for spirals (10–20cm)
- 26-gauge sterling or fine-silver sheet for spacers (1.5x6cm)
- 24-gauge sterling or fine-silver sheet for bead caps (2x2cm)
- 0.021" and 0.024" diameter multi-strand beading wire
- 2 silver bead caps
- 4–6 sterling silver crimp beads, 1mm
- 2 sterling silver crimp bead covers, 3.2mm
- 2 sterling silver wire guards (optional)

BEADS
- 13mm Bali-style silver bead
- 10–12 gemstone beads such as phrenite, ruby, grossular garnet, or jade, 4–20mm
- 6–8 faceted gemstone beads (garnet, peridot, iolite) for dangles and beaded loop, 3–4mm
- 10–14 seed beads or 1–2mm semi-precious stone faceted beads for beaded loop
- 3–4 round sterling silver beads, 2mm
- 3–4 silver spacers, 1cm diameter
- 20–24 silver spacers, 2–3mm diameter
- Silver charm, 4–5mm (optional)

At first glance, this bracelet appears to be a fairly straightforward design, but a closer look reveals handmade nuances that customize the whole piece. Findings are fabricated from silver sheet and wire, and the balled-wire rings are an easy starter torchwork project.

The bracelet combines some really juicy semiprecious stone beads with Bali-style granulated silver spacers and bead caps, and is perfect for displaying a special lampwork bead.

DESIGN NOTE

This bracelet is a little longer than usual to accommodate all the large beads. The two balled-end rings were soldered closed, but if you'd like to skip the torchwork, you can wrap the ends tightly back around the ring to secure them.

Finished length: 21cm

template

Make two flower bead caps

Using the template provided, trace two flowers onto 24-gauge fine silver or sterling silver sheet. Use a 4/0 or 5/0 blade to saw out the shapes. File the edges as needed. Smooth the edges with an extra-fine knife-edge wheel. Sand the surfaces to remove any edge burrs with 320-grit silicon carbide sandpaper, and finish with 400-grit polishing paper. Drill the center of each flower with a #60 high-speed twist drill bit. Use a small circle stamp or other design for the surface embellishment. Antique with liver of sulfur and polish with 400-grit polishing paper.

Dome the flower bead caps

Use a metal dapping punch set to dome the flowers into bead caps. Use punches in these approximate sizes: 16mm, 14mm, 12mm, and 11mm. Depending on the size of the bead you are using, you may need to change the size of the punches to fit the bead appropriately.

For each bead cap: Find a depression in the dapping block that is just large enough to allow the largest dapping punch to fit **[A]**. Center the flower face down in the depression, set the punch on the flower, and strike the punch with a utility hammer. Remove the bead cap and place it in a depression that fits the next-smallest punch (14mm). Repeat the doming process using 12mm and 11mm punches. Polish the surfaces of each bead cap with the 400-grit polishing paper. This photo shows a finished cap next to a cap before it was domed **[B]**.

Prepare the clasp

Cut 7.5cm of 16-gauge sterling silver wire. Smooth both ends of the wire with a file and an extra-fine abrasive wheel. Use chainnose or roundnose pliers to turn a 1½-revolution spiral in the end. If the pliers mar the wire, use an abrasive wheel to buff out the marks. Use a narrow mandrel to form the curve of the clasp **[C]**. Make a second spiral at the end of the wire, spiraling it in the reverse direction **[D]** and leaving a 2mm opening. Continue

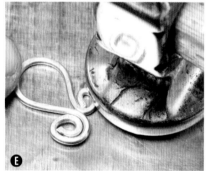

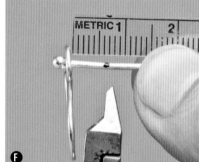

the spiral almost two full revolutions. Forge the whole clasp with a chasing hammer **[E]**. Use an extra-fine abrasive wheel to remove any hammer marks. Use 400-grit polishing paper on both sides of the clasp until the surface is uniform.

Ball wire for the clasp

Measure and cut 4cm of 16-gauge fine-silver wire. Use a jumbo butane torch to ball one end of the wire large enough so that it will not pull through the larger spiral end of the clasp. String the

balled wire in the larger clasp spiral and measure 6–7mm past the spiral **[F]**. Trim the wire. Suspend the balled wire through the larger spiral. Hold the spiral with tweezers and ball up the lower end of the wire, being careful to avoid melting the spiral **[G]**. The balled wire should move freely in the spiral when finished. Quench. If the piece oxidized from too much heat, pickle it and rinse. Polish both sides of the clasp with 400-grit polishing paper to remove any scratches.

Make two balled-end rings

Cut two 6cm pieces of 16-gauge fine-silver wire. Make a small balled end on one end of each wire. Wrap each wire around a 8mm diameter mandrel, starting from the center of the wire and working out to the ends. Leave 1cm at each end of the wire extending straight out from the coil. Hold the ring in tweezers with the ends vertical and ball the other end of each wire **[H]**.

For each ring: Finish wrapping the balled ends around the mandrel. The ends won't form a full second revolution. Place the single-wire side of the ring on the corner of a bench block and use a chasing hammer to lightly forge that section to flatten it. Wrap each balled wire end down and a bit around the outside of the loop to help secure the ends around the loop. Although you can use the rings as they are, soldering the balled ends to the rings in the next step creates a more-solid ring.

Solder the ends to the ring

For each ring: Clean and cut some easy or extra-easy solder. Use a butane torch to lightly heat the ring. Apply a thin, even coat of flux and heat until dry. Dip the end of a fine-tip paintbrush in flux, dab off the excess, pick up a solder pallion, and place it in the crease between each beaded wire end and the loop **[I]**. Lightly heat the solder board in a circular motion around the ring for 10–15 seconds without letting the flame touch the ring.

Bring the end of the flame closer to the ring for 5–10 seconds. Move the torch low and to the front of the solder board, moving it back and forth across the ring **[J]**. Both pieces of solder should flow. Quench, pickle, rinse, and dry.

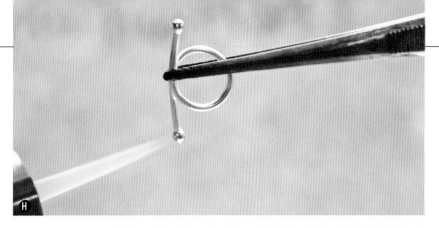

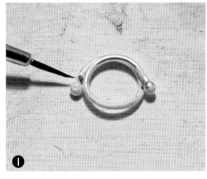

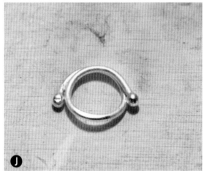

Use an extra-fine abrasive knife-edge or wheel to clean up any excess solder. Use a 400-grit (blue) bristle disk to remove any remaining oxidation and put a uniform finish on the two rings.

Polish the clasp and rings

Tumble-polish the clasp and two rings for 30–60 minutes, or use a felt wheel and polishing compound to polish the pieces.

Prepare silver spacers

I interspersed a few disks and wire spirals as spacers between some of the beads. Make a few 10–15mm spirals from 20-gauge sterling or fine-silver wire. Use a disk cutter to make some 10–15mm 26-gauge sterling or fine-silver disks. Drill holes in the centers of the disks with a #60 drill bit. Texture and antique the pieces if desired. Buff and polish them with extra-fine abrasive wheels and 400-grit polishing paper.

Prepare the gemstone bead spacers

Cut two 4cm pieces of 24-gauge fine-silver wire and make a small ball on one end of each wire. Straighten and work-harden the wires by rolling them between two bench blocks. String 10–14 gemstone or seed beads onto each wire. Form the balled wire into a small ring, leaving a bit of wire exposed next to the balled end. Coil the loose end of the wire around the exposed neck of the balled wire end several times **[K]**. Trim the extra wire.

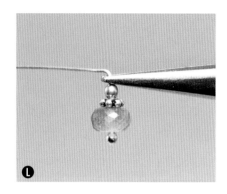

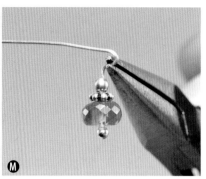

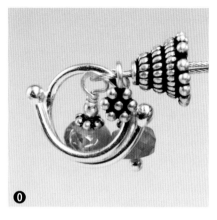

Make four bead dangles

With a butane torch, ball one end of four 5cm pieces of 24-gauge fine-silver wire. Roll the wires between two bench blocks. Polish lightly with a piece of 400-grit polishing paper.

For each dangle: String a faceted gemstone bead, a silver spacer, and a 2mm round silver bead onto a wire. Holding the wire directly above the round bead with chainnose pliers, bend the wire 90 degrees over the pliers jaw **[L]**. Grasp the wire just past the bend and wrap the wire around the jaw to make a loop **[M]**. Move the pliers to grasp the top of the loop and wrap the wire down and around to coil around the vertical wire neck **[N]**. Finish the coil and trim the excess wire. Polish the loop with a polishing stick.

Assemble the long section of the bracelet

The section of large beads in this bracelet is about 14.5cm long. String the beads and spacers onto a piece of beading wire to determine which order works best. You may choose to dome some of the spacers so they fit better alongside certain beads. If any of the gemstone bead holes are too small, enlarge them with a bead reamer or a tapered drill bit followed by a cylinder diamond drill bit.

String a soldered jump ring onto a 25cm piece of 0.024" beading wire about 3–4cm from the end of the wire. Add two bead dangles and a small silver charm (optional). String both ends of the wire through a bead cap. Adjust the jump ring so that the single-wire side of the jump ring is closest to the bead cap **[O]**. String one or two crimp beads onto both ends of the wire. Push the crimp beads up into the bead cap and flatten the crimp beads with chainnose pliers. The bead cap hides the crimp beads. Trim the short end of the wire below the crimp beads.

String the beads

String the remainder of the beads. Here is the order of components in my bracelet: soldered ring with two bead dangles and a silver charm, bead cap, silver disk, grossular garnet rectangle, silver spiral, three ruby spacers, silver disk, phrenite faceted bead, silver spacer, seed bead loop, large Bali-style bead, ruby spacer, silver disk, ruby faceted bead, silver spacer, silver disk, lampwork glass bead, silver disk, bead cap, ruby, bead cap, garnet loop, round jade bead, bead cap, crimp bead(s), and a soldered ring with a bead dangle. The length of this section of beads, including the two rings, is 16.5cm.

Pass the beading wire around the ring, back though the bead cap, and into the crimp bead(s). Flatten the crimp bead(s) with chainnose pliers or use a crimping pliers. Trim the wire.

Assemble the small beaded loop

The length of the gemstone bead loop is about 4cm without the clasp. On 0.021" beading wire, string an arrangement of gemstone beads and silver spacers. String a crimp bead on each end. On one end, string a gemstone bead dangle. String both ends through the small loop of the clasp, add a wire guard if desired, and go back through the crimp beads. Close each crimp bead with crimping pliers. Trim the excess wire and cover each crimp bead with a crimp cover. ■

RIVETED BEAD STACK
earrings

In this project, you'll set a tube rivet within a stack of beads so the stack stays neatly together but can turn around the earring wire. You'll also practice enlarging holes in your beads. You'll make two stamped silver squares to use as bead caps and two silver spirals for spacers.

TOOLKITS
- Cutting
- Filing
- Finishing
- Drilling
- Forming & Forging
- Antiquing
- Tube-riveting
- Torchwork

MATERIALS
- 26-gauge sterling silver sheet (2x8cm)
- 18-gauge sterling silver wire for earring wires (16–20cm)
- 16-gauge sterling silver or fine-silver wire for spiral (16cm)
- 2.57mm OD sterling silver tubing (6–8cm; varies based on height of bead stack)

BEADS
- 6 pairs of assorted disk beads, 6–12mm

DESIGN NOTE

Choose disk beads that are thin and not perfectly round to make your bead stacks interesting. Test which beads lie well together by stringing them on a headpin. Consider the weight of the earrings as you choose beads; amber and shell are lightweight relative to gemstone beads. My earrings use pairs of Chinese turquoise, amber, brown glass, and dyed red coral.

Finished length: 6cm

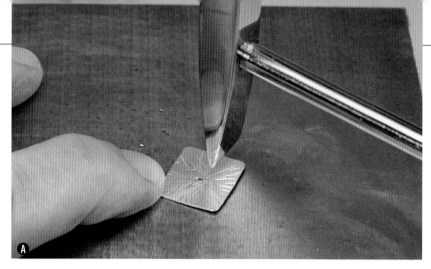

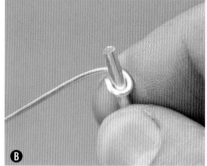

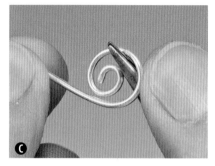

Prepare silver spacers

Cut or saw three pairs of spacer shapes out of 26-gauge sterling silver sheet. Consider square, rectangular, oval, or round based on what works best with your beads. My spacers are 15x16mm and 10x10mm. Base the size of the largest spacer on the diameter of the bottom bead in the stack.

File off sharp corners and use an abrasive wheel to buff and bevel the edges of the spacers. Sand both sides with 400-grit polishing paper until the surfaces are uniform. Texture the spacers as desired; I used the cross-peen face of a riveting hammer **[A]**.

Make two coiled spirals

Cut two 8cm pieces of 16-gauge fine-silver or sterling silver wire. Flush-cut one end of each wire and smooth the sharp edges with a sanding stick or an extra-fine or fine abrasive wheel.

For each spiral: Make a small coil around a piece of 2.57mm tubing using chainnose or roundnose pliers **[B]**. Continue to add to the spiral up to two full revolutions using roundnose pliers or the outside of the chainnose pliers jaw **[C]**. I made a 13mm spiral; base the size on the size of the bead that will lie below it in the stack. Use the domed face of a chasing or planishing hammer to lightly flatten the

spiral. Cut off the wire end at an angle. Use an extra-fine abrasive wheel to smooth the wire end. Sand the spiral on a piece of 400-grit polishing paper until the surface is uniform.

Drill the center of each spacer

For each spacer: Create a dimple in the center with a center punch and drill a hole with a #60 drill bit. Use a 2.3mm (³⁄₃₂") carbide drill bit to enlarge each hole **[D]**. Test a piece of 2.57mm tubing for fit. Enlarge the hole with a round needle file until the tubing snugly fits the hole. Sand off any burrs on the back.

Antique and dome the spacers

Antique the spacers with liver of sulfur and use superfine steel wool to remove the excess patina. Use a shallow wood dapping punch and block to dome each disk slightly.

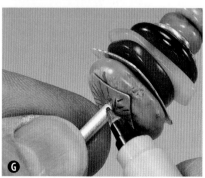

⚠ **SAFETY** Use a GFCI outlet with the rotary tool for drilling underwater.

Enlarge the bead holes

You will most likely need to enlarge the bead holes to allow the tubing to fit. For each bead, start with a tapered diamond bit to enlarge the hole slightly on each side **[E]**. You don't need to work underwater because you'll drill for only a few seconds. Change to a 2.5mm hollow-core diamond drill bit and place the bead on a small wood block submerged in a small dish of water **[F]**. Drill through the bead. Check the fit of each bead on the tubing; it should fit snugly. If the bead does not fit on the tubing, use the hollow-core bit to open the hole by pressing the bit into the wall of the bead in a circular motion as you drill.

Cut and anneal the tubing

For each bead stack: Arrange the beads and spacers on the tubing. Push the top of the bead stack to one end of the tubing. Leave a length of tubing exposed above the stack equal to half the diameter of the tubing. I left about 1.25mm since the tubing diameter is 2.57mm. Below the stack, mark the tubing about the same distance from the bottom of the silver spacer **[G]**. Use a jeweler's saw or a tube cutter to cut the tubing just outside of the mark. Sand off any burrs at both ends of the tubing. Sand both ends of the tubing with 400-grit polishing paper until they are flat and uniform. Use a round needle file to clear out any burrs in the hole at each end.

To easily form the rivet collar, use a micro butane torch to anneal both pieces of tubing to a dull red cherry glow. Quench. Remove any surface oxidation by pickling or using a piece of 400-grit polishing paper.

Set the tube rivet

For each bead stack: Place the beads on the tube and place the stack on a metal bench block. Place the end of a 3mm center punch into the top of the tube and lightly strike the punch a few times with a hammer to flare the top of the tube **[H]**. Turn the stack over, center the beads on the tube, and repeat on the bottom **[I]**. Repeat top and bottom until the beads are held in place on the tube by the flared ends. Repeat this process with a steel dapping punch (5–8mm wide). Work back and forth from top to bottom until the tube collar starts to roll over **[J]**. Don't forget to strike the flaring tools lightly with the hammer and be patient!

Finish the rivet collar

For each bead stack: Cover the top bead and bottom spacer with painters tape to prevent hammer marks. Use the ball-peen end of a chasing hammer to finish rolling over the edge of the tubing **[K]**. Work at eye level with the bead stack so you can see where on the collar the edge starts to roll over. Work all around the edge of the rivet. Polish the rivet collar with a 400-grit polishing stick or use an extra-fine abrasive wheel to smooth each collar until the surface is uniform. Remove the tape.

Form the earring wires

Ball one end of each of two 8–10cm pieces of 18-gauge fine-silver wire. Flatten the face of each balled end lightly with a chasing hammer. Antique the wire with liver of sulfur solution and use 400-grit polishing paper to remove some of the patina. Insert a wire into each bead stack.

For each earring wire: Mark the point on the wire that you would like for the total earring height. Remove the bead stack. Place the wire on a bench block with the flat face of the balled end facing up and extending off the side of the block. Use a chasing hammer to lightly forge along the wire from the balled end to just below the mark **[L]**. Sand both faces of the wire lightly with 400-grit polishing paper. String a bead stack on the wire. Form the top of the earring wire using a narrow mandrel such as a pen or wood dowel. Finish forming the back of the wire and trim the excess wire. Use a chasing hammer to forge the back of the wire. Use 400-grit polishing paper to buff the earring wire surfaces. Smooth the cut wire end. The bead stack will move up and down freely on the wire. ∎

ETCHED EARRINGS
with turquoise

These sterling silver earrings can feature any large drilled rondelle (I used Chinese turquoise) or even a lampwork glass bead. The disks are etched with a freehand design. This earring style is easy to modify; see the photos of my variations on p. 60 for a few ideas to get you started.

TOOLKITS
- Cutting (disk cutter)
- Filing
- Finishing
- Forming & Forging
- Drilling
- Antiquing
- Etching (ferric nitrate etchant)
- Torchwork

ADDITIONAL SUPPLIES
- Drafting template (circles)

MATERIALS
- 24-gauge sterling silver sheet (1" wide strip; length determined by size of disks)
- 18- or 20-gauge sterling silver or fine-silver wire (16–24cm, depending on desired earring length)

BEADS
- 2 rondelle beads, about 10x18mm

Finished length: 5.5cm

Cut the disks
Use a disk cutter to cut five disks out of a 1" wide strip of 24-gauge sterling silver or fine silver. The size of the disk is a matter of personal preference: Decide if you would like a slightly larger disk as a means to display a detailed design, which will cover up more of the bead, or a smaller disk that will show more of the bead. I made 14mm diameter disks for my 18mm diameter beads **[A]**.

TIP I usually cut an extra disk when I create a freehand design; not all of my etching results are perfect, so preparing an extra disk allows me to choose the disks that look best together.

Clean and sand the disks
Wash off any residual cutting lubricant with soapy water. Sand each disk on 320-grit silicon carbide sandpaper to remove any edge burrs. Sand with 400-grit sandpaper or polishing paper until the disk surfaces are uniform.

Mark the disk centers
Mark the disk center and incorporate this point as part of the inked resist design. When the etched disk is drilled, the metal will remain thick at the center. An easy way to mark the centerpoint is to align each disk with the grid lines on a circle template and lightly mark the crosshair lines **[B]**. Mark the centerpoint and remove the lines with a 400-grit polishing stick.

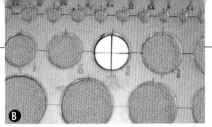

Prepare the etching design

For each disk: Use a fine-tip permanent marker to trace a design on one side of the metal. Use a thicker marker to trace a thick border. After the ink dries, use nail polish to trace over the marker lines **[C]**; the photo shows a design in marker only (left) and with nail polish overlay. It's important to apply resist to the entire outside edge of each disk **[D]**.

Etching setup

Place the disks pattern side up on the sticky side of a 12" piece of electrical tape with at least ½" between each disk. Make sure that each disk is fully backed by the tape. Burnish the back of each disk with your fingernail.

Etch the disks

Refer to Etching, p. 25, for detailed directions. Place the disks in the solution as directed. For sterling silver, check the progress in about 2 hours and again at 3 hours and subsequently in shorter time increments. You should see some progress by 3 hours. My disks were left in the etching solution for 4 hours.

Remove the disks from the tape, neutralize them, and rinse well with water. Use acetone or denatured alcohol to remove any remaining nail polish and ink. The recessed areas will probably be discolored at this point. Use a brass brush or a 400-grit radial bristle disk to remove any oxidation or residual nail polish in the recessed design **[E]**; the photo shows the disks before brushing (top) and after.

Drill the disk centers

For each disk: Make a dimple on the centerpoint with a center punch and drill a hole using a #60 high-speed twist drill bit. Smooth the burr on the back of each disk with sandpaper.

Check the size of the holes

Check the fit of the earring wire in each drilled hole. If necessary, use a round

needle file to enlarge the hole just enough to allow the wire to fit; you want a tight fit around the wire.

Antique the disks

Antique the disks with liver of sulfur. Use superfine steel wool to lightly buff the disks and highlight the design.

Dome the disks

Use wood and metal dapping block sets to dome the best four disks, and save the odd disk to use as a bracelet or necklace charm. Start with a shallow depression in the wood dapping block. Check the fit with a bead. If the dome is not deep enough to fit, dap again in a deeper depression.

Prepare the earring wires

Choose the thickness of wire suited for the size of the beads and earring length. If the beads are large or if you want a long earring, use 18-gauge wire.

DESIGN NOTE

In most of my projects that call for etching sterling silver, you can substitute economical nickel silver and use ferric chloride as the etchant. Etched and antiqued nickel silver looks nearly identical to antiqued sterling silver. Note that some people have skin sensitivities to nickel silver.

For a short (4cm) earring, cut about 16cm of wire. For a long (6.25cm) earring, cut 24cm of wire. Cut the wire in half.

Ball the wire ends

Use a torch to ball one end of each earring wire. The ball should be large enough to not pull through the drilled disk hole. If you use sterling silver wire, use an abrasive wheel to remove pits and oxidation.

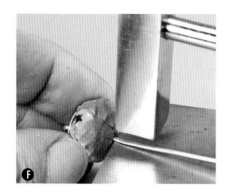

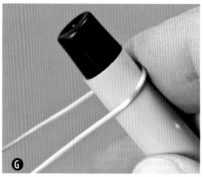

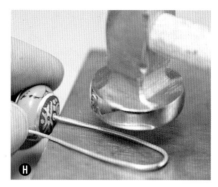

Straighten the earring wires

Place each earring wire between two metal bench blocks with the balled end exposed. Roll the top block back and forth to straighten and work-harden the wire.

Assemble the earrings

For each earring: String a disk, a bead, and a disk on a wire. To protect the metal disk from hammer nicks, place small pieces of painters tape over the disk. Place the assembly off the edge of a metal bench block and lightly forge the wire right above the bead using the flat head of a riveting hammer **[F]**. Make the wire just wide enough so the top disk can't move on the wire.

Form the earring wires

With the flattened sides of the wire facing out, form the top curve of each earring wire around a mandrel such as a pen or marker **[G]**. Check the earrings to make sure they are the same length. If not, shorten the longer earring by pulling the top curve tighter around the form. (You can also use a larger round form such as a prescription pill bottle to curve the whole length of each wire.) Use a chasing hammer to lightly forge along the full length of the wires to widen them **[H]**. Trim the ends of each wire and make a small outward bend behind the bead. Smooth the wires with a 400-grit polishing stick.

Antique the earring wires

If you like, the earring wires can be antiqued at this point. Buff off the patina as desired. If you want a high shine, buff the metal disks and earring wires with a polishing stick. Wash the earrings with soapy water, rinse, and dry. ∎

variations

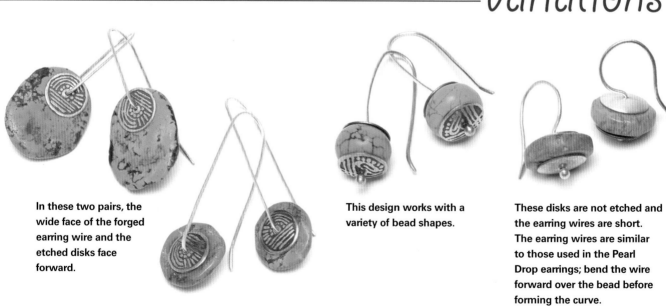

In these two pairs, the wide face of the forged earring wire and the etched disks face forward.

This design works with a variety of bead shapes.

These disks are not etched and the earring wires are short. The earring wires are similar to those used in the Pearl Drop earrings; bend the wire forward over the bead before forming the curve.

MIXED METAL *pendant*

This pendant project features sterling silver and copper elements. Both pieces are etched with simple repeated geometric shapes. Sterling silver wire rivets secure the copper bail that suspends a coin pearl.

I soldered chain ends onto ball chain and added a clasp, but you can hang the pendant from any type of readymade necklace chain.

TOOLKITS

• Cutting
• Drilling
• Filing
• Finishing
• Etching (ferric nitrate etchant)
• Antiquing
• Forming & Forging
• Torchwork

MATERIALS

• 20- or 22-gauge sterling silver sheet (4.5x4.5cm)
• 24-gauge copper sheet (5.5x2cm)
• 14-gauge fine-silver wire (1.5cm)
• 20-gauge fine-silver wire (3cm)
• 2.5–3mm sterling silver ball chain (61cm)
• Sterling silver lobster claw clasp and jump rings
• 2 sterling silver chain end caps

BEAD

• Freshwater pearl: coin shape or round, 10–12mm diameter

Finished width: 4cm

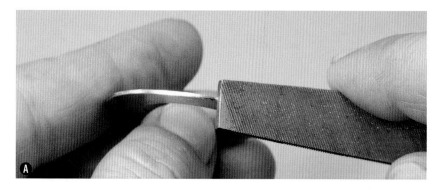

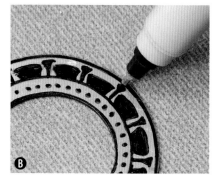

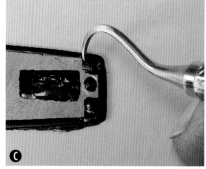

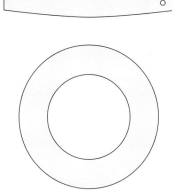

templates

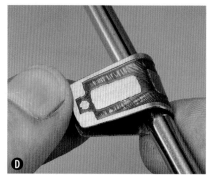

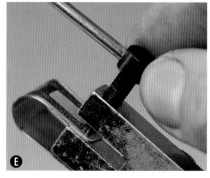

Prepare the silver disk

Trace the donut-shaped template onto 20- or 22-gauge sterling silver sheet. Use a 2/0 saw blade to saw out the disk. Pierce the center of the circle with a drill bit and saw out the inner circle. Use a coarse hand file to smooth the outer edge of the circle by filing first in one direction and then in the opposite direction **[A]**. Remove burrs with 320-grit silicon carbide sandpaper.

Prepare the copper bail

Trace the bail template onto 24-gauge copper sheet. Use a 5/0 or 6/0 saw blade to saw out the shape. Remove burrs with 320-grit silicon carbide sandpaper.

Prepare the etching patterns

Apply a resist design to the silver disk and the copper bail. On my disk, I used markers to draw repeating motifs **[B]**. I added an extra layer of nail polish resist to create a bolder pattern in certain areas. On the copper bail, I reinforced the entire marker resist design with nail polish before etching. Use a dental tool or toothpick to remove stray nail polish **[C]**.

Etch the metal

See Etching, p. 25, for specific directions on etching the silver disk in ferric nitrate for 3–4 hours. Etch the copper bail in ferric chloride for 1¼–1½ hours. Neutralize both pieces, clean them with acetone, and use an extra-fine abrasive wheel to polish and bevel the edges. Use a 400-grit bristle disk to remove the stain on the etched areas until the metal is shiny.

Antique the metal pieces

Antique both pieces in liver of sulfur. Remove the excess patina with 400-grit polishing paper or superfine steel wool.

Fold over the bail

Fold the bail over a narrow mandrel such as a riveting hammer handle **[D]**. Adjust the bail ends so that they are aligned. The copper will fold over easily since it is thinner after etching.

Make the bail holes

Mark and center three dots in a row at the front lower lip of the bail, approximately 2–3mm from the edge. The pearl will be suspended from the center hole and the outer holes will be used for the wire rivets. Open the bail slightly and align the ¹⁄₁₆" screw-action punch over a dot **[E]**. Make three holes in the front of the bail.

Pinch the lower 2cm of the bail ends together until they touch and are aligned evenly. Place the bail into the punch and wind the screw into one of the outer holes. Screw though the hole into the back of the bail to make a hole. Remove the bail from the punch and insert a piece of 14-gauge wire into this first pair of holes. The wire helps to keep the bail ends and pairs of holes aligned. With the bail ends aligned, use the screw punch to make a hole in the back of the bail on the

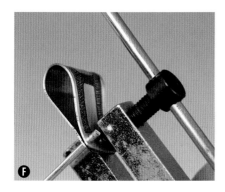

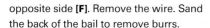

opposite side **[F]**. Remove the wire. Sand the back of the bail to remove burrs.

Prepare the wire for riveting

Sand one end of a piece of 14-gauge fine-silver wire flat. Pinch the bail ends together tightly and insert the wire into the edge holes on one side of the bail. Because 14-gauge wire is about 1.6mm wide, you'll need to have a bit less than 1mm (0.8mm or half the diameter) of wire extending at both sides of the bail. With 0.8mm of wire extending from the front, use a fine-tip marker to mark the same length on the back **[G]**. (The diameter of a fine-tip marker point is usually about that size.) Cut just outside of the mark with fine-tip wire cutters. My wire was 3mm long; the length of yours will depend on the thickness of your etched copper. Hold the wire upright with chainnose pliers and sand the other end flat. Prepare a second piece of wire for the opposite edge holes.

Set the rivets

Insert the silver ring into the bail. Use painters tape to protect the ends of the bail from hammer nicks. Insert one prepared piece of wire into one set of holes. Use the cross-peen face of a riveting hammer to flare the end over the bail **[H]**. Flip the assembly over on the bench block. Make sure the wire is still evenly seated from top to bottom in the hole. Flare the opposite end of the wire. Work back and forth until both ends are flared. Switch to the ball end of a chasing

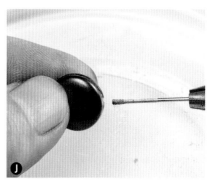

hammer to roll the outside edge of the rivet heads down **[I]**. Set the second rivet into the opposite holes in the same way.

Finish the rivets

Use an extra-fine abrasive wheel or bullet end to polish the rivet heads. If desired, dab on a bit of liver of sulfur solution to darken the rivet heads. Buff the rivet heads.

⚠ **SAFETY Use a GFCI outlet with the rotary tool for drilling underwater.**

Drill the pearl

Use a set of thin-shaft diamond drill bits to enlarge the pearl's hole underwater **[J]**.

Attach the pearl

Ball one end of a 2–3cm piece of 20-gauge fine-silver wire. String the pearl on the wire. Make a tiny loop above the pearl and string the wire through the bail. Bend the loop down and over the back of the bail to make a simple U-shaped hook. Antique the wire and buff.

Prepare and attach a chain

Any type of sterling silver or copper chain can be used for this necklace. I used easy solder to attach end caps to 2.5mm sterling ball chain (see the Riveted Beach Stone Bracelet, p. 74, for detailed instructions). An option is to use a prefabricated necklace chain. Antique the chain, clasp, and jump rings. String the chain through the bail. ■

DESIGN NOTE

Nickel silver can be substituted for sterling silver in this project; follow etching and antiquing directions for nickel silver. Or, instead of etching the disk and bail, consider creating surface texture with tools such as design stamps or hammers.

RIVETED & ETCHED *spinner ring*

Put a spectacular bead on display in an open-ended ring band secured by a tube rivet. You can control whether the bead spins as you set the tube rivet; some beads, like this flattened pumpkin shape, work better fixed in place.

TOOLKITS
- Drilling
- Torchwork
- Cutting
- Finishing
- Etching (ferric nitrate etchant)
- Antiquing
- Filing
- Forming & Forging
- Tube-Riveting

ADDITIONAL TOOLS & SUPPLIES
- Firm cardstock
- Wide-shank finger gauge set for ring sizing

MATERIALS
- 2.57mm sterling silver tubing (5cm)
- 20-gauge sterling silver sheet (approximately 2x10cm; will vary with ring size)

BEAD
- Focal bead, about 2.5mm

DESIGN NOTES

You'll probably need to enlarge the hole in your bead to fit the tubing, but it's likely that the channel will be too long to be drilled with a hollow-core bit; the bead will get stuck on the shaft, which is wider than the diamond end of the bit. Use a solid-shaft diamond bit instead.

The template is for a ring of about size 9. You may need to enlarge or reduce the length of the band after testing the fit.

In many projects, you can substitute nickel silver for sterling silver, but for this ring, stick with sterling silver for its malleability. Nickel silver is stiff and difficult to form.

template

Finished band width: 13–16mm

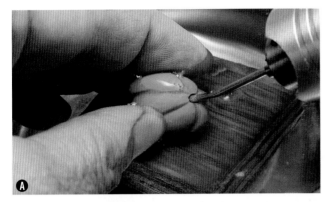

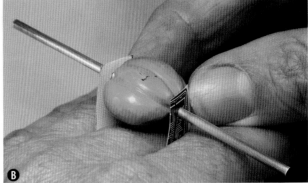

⚠ SAFETY Use a GFCI outlet with the rotary tool for drilling underwater.

Drill the bead

Use a 2.5mm solid-shaft diamond drill bit to enlarge the bead hole underwater **[A]**. Test the fit of the tubing. If the hole is too small, press the drill bit against the wall of the hole in a circular motion while drilling to widen it.

Anneal the tubing

Anneal about 5cm of 2.57mm sterling silver tubing.

Prepare the template

Trace the template onto cardstock and cut it out. Use an awl or drill bit to make a hole in each end. Insert the tubing into the bead and fit the tubing into the holes on the template band **[B]**.

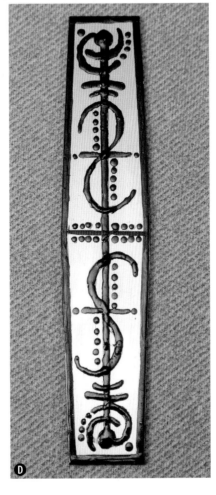

The final length of the band will depend on your finger/ring size as well as the thickness of the bead. Determine the best position of the tubing hole for a good fit and add about 1mm to accommodate the thickness of the metal sheet. The final position of the holes should be about 3mm from the template ends; make them closer to the ends if you have a particularly thick bead. Adjust the template as necessary.

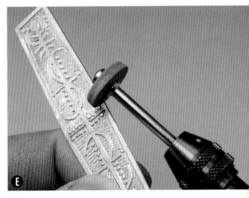

Cut out the metal band

Trace the template onto the 20-gauge silver sheet and cut it out using a 2/0 saw blade. Sand both sides with 320-grit silicon carbide sandpaper to remove burrs.

Create the resist and etch the band

Mark a 1mm border **[C]**. Use permanent markers to draw a design on the band. Fill the border with resist as well. Trace over the marker design with nail polish to create a better resist **[D]**. Etch the band in ferric nitrate for 2–3 hours, checking the progress every 30 minutes starting at one hour (see Etching, p. 25, for detailed instructions). Neutralize. Use acetone to remove the nail polish. Any stained areas can be cleaned with a 400-grit bristle disk. Use an extra-fine abrasive wheel to smooth any nicks on the edges. Bevel the top and bottom of the band to make it comfortable to wear **[E]**.

Antique the band

Antique the band with liver of sulfur and buff with 400-grit polishing paper. Use superfine steel wool to highlight the high areas and remove some patina in the recesses.

DESIGN NOTE

If you don't have a set of finger gauges to measure your ring size, wrap the cardstock template around your finger and tape it to hold at the right size. Put the taped template over your ring mandrel to estimate where to work to form the band.

Drill the rivet holes

Use a center punch to make a dimple for each hole. Use a #52–60 high-speed twist drill bit to make a set hole; use a 3/32" (2.3mm) carbide or high-speed twist drill bit to finish drilling each hole. Sand the back of the band with 320-grit silicon carbide sandpaper to remove burrs. The holes should be slightly smaller than the tubing at this point. Use a round needle file to slowly enlarge the holes until the tubing fits snugly.

Form the band

Place the band at the position on a ring mandrel that approximates your ring size. Slowly bend both ends of the band simultaneously around the mandrel until the ends of the band are parallel to one another **[F]**. Tap the band lightly with a rawhide or nylon mallet to form it to size if necessary.

Cut the tubing

Sand one end of the tubing until it is flat. Insert the sanded end into the hole on one side of the band, through the bead, and out the other side of the band.

Adjust the tubing so that one end extends approximately 1–1.25mm from the outside of one side of the band. Pinch the ends of the band against the bead. On the opposite side of the ring, make a mark about 1mm from the side of the band **[G]**. Remove the tubing, saw off the end at the mark, and sand the end flat to remove any burrs.

Set the rivet

If you want your bead to spin freely, use a business card as a temporary spacer: Make a hole in two small pieces of the card and place these spacers on the tube between the bead and the ring band. Assemble the tube, bead, and band again, centering the tube so an equal length is exposed on each side of the band.

Place the assembly on a bench block and use a center punch to flare both ends of the tube **[H]**. Make sure the tube stays centered on the ring band. Use a metal dapping punch (6mm–8mm) to roll the tube ends over. If you used card spacers, remove them (wetting them if necessary).

Cover the band around each collar with painters tape to prevent nicks, and finish forming the collars with a chasing hammer **[I]**. Smooth both collars with an extra-fine abrasive wheel. ∎

CORAL CLAMSHELL
necklace

This pendant design allows the color of a wide coral bead to peek out beneath an etched disk. The bead is cradled in a textured and domed sterling silver disk.

DESIGN NOTE

Copper or nickel silver are good substitutes for sterling silver in this project. Use ferric chloride as the etchant.

TOOLKITS
- Cutting (disk cutter)
- Etching (ferric nitrate etchant)
- Finishing
- Drilling
- Filing
- Annealing
- Forming & Forging
- Torchwork

MATERIALS
- 24-gauge sterling silver sheet (4.5x4.5cm)
- 26-gauge sterling silver sheet (2x2cm)
- 18-gauge square sterling silver wire (20cm)
- 18-gauge sterling silver wire (3cm)
- 2.57mm OD sterling silver tubing (2–3cm)
- 3.9mm rolo-style sterling silver chain (72cm)
- Sterling silver lobster claw clasp
- 2 5mm oval jump rings

BEADS
- 2 coral beads (7mm and 24mm diameter)

Finished pendant
width: 4cm

THREE-RING CORAL
earrings

For this project, you'll make three sizes of rings and use four different types of solder to make the joins, starting with high-temperature solder for the first join and finishing with the lowest-temperature solder.

TOOLKITS
• Cutting
• Finishing
• Drilling
• Torchwork
• Forming & Forging
• Filing

MATERIALS
• 26-gauge sterling or fine-silver sheet (approximately 2x6cm)
• 18-gauge fine-silver round wire (8–10cm)
• 20-gauge sterling silver round wire (3cm)
• 18-gauge sterling silver square wire (70cm)
• 2 sterling silver earring wire clutch nuts

BEADS
• 2 coral or turquoise disk beads, approximately 20mm wide x 5–7mm tall

Finished length: 5cm

Prepare the disks
Use a disk cutter to cut four disks from a strip of 26-gauge sterling silver (annealing the metal first is not necessary). Sand both sides of each disk on 320-grit sandpaper until both sides have a uniform finish. If any edges are not flat, flatten them on a metal bench block with a rawhide mallet. Sand both sides of each disk with 400-grit sandpaper until uniform in appearance. Use an extra-fine abrasive wheel to polish and smooth the edges of each disk.

Drill a hole in the center of each disk with a #60 high-speed twist drill bit. Test the size of the holes with a piece of 18-gauge wire and use the end of a round needle file to enlarge the holes if necessary. Sand off the burr on the back of each disk with 400-grit sandpaper. Use a shallow cup of the wood dapping block to lightly dome each disk **[A]**. Sand each disk lightly with fine-grit polishing paper or extra-fine steel wool to a satin finish.

Prepare the balled-end wires
Cut two 4cm pieces of 18-gauge fine-silver round wire. Ball one end of each wire with a butane torch until the balls are the same size.

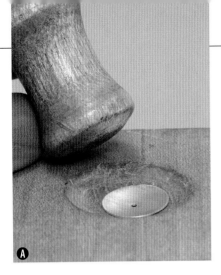

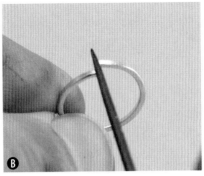

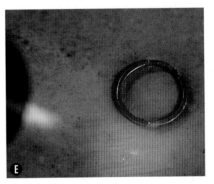

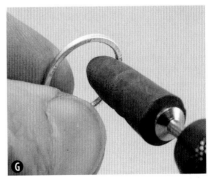

Anneal the square wire

Gently wrap 40cm of 18-gauge sterling silver square wire into a loose coil about 10cm in diameter. Use a jumbo butane torch to anneal the wire. Quench, pickle, rinse, and dry.

Make the square wire rings

Open the coil of annealed wire and straighten the wire. Remove any minor twists from the square wire so that it lies fairly flat. Use wood dowels in three sizes (7mm, 9mm, and 12mm) and follow the instructions on p. 30 to make four or five rings in each size. (You will need just two in each size for this project; set the others aside.) Don't use beeswax as you saw; it could interfere with soldering.

File and close the jump ring ends

Use the flat side of a needle file or 320-grit sandpaper to remove the burrs at each end of each ring [B]. Use two chainnose pliers to close each ring so the ends are perfectly flush with no visible gap [C]. If necessary, use a combination flatnose/half-round pliers to work the ends closed.

Place two 12mm rings on a solder board. Lightly heat each ring with the torch and lightly coat both sides with flux. Continue heating until the flux dries. If the dried flux is uneven, rinse, dry, and reapply.

Solder the 12mm rings closed

Clean and cut small pallions of the four types of solder wire (hard, medium, easy, and extra-easy). Keep them separated and identified. Place a small pallion of hard solder at the inside edge of each 12mm ring's seam [D].

Use a butane torch to solder each seam closed: Move the outer tip of the flame in a circle over the ring for 5–10 seconds without touching the ring. Bring the tip of the blue inner cone closer to the ring and quickly circle the flame directly over the ring.

When the flux changes from powdery white to clear, move the flame to the outer edge of the ring in front of the pallion. Move the flame slightly back and forth at this position. The ring will turn a dull reddish orange color and the solder pallion will turn molten and flow across the seam [E].

Pick up the ring with metal tweezers and flip it over on the board. While the ring is still hot, spray it lightly again with flux. Reheat the ring and, as the flux clears, move the flame directly above the join until the molten solder pulls up through the seam to the top of the ring. Quench, pickle, rinse, and dry.

If either ring has gray blotches or excess solder, use an extra-fine abrasive wheel to clean the surfaces [F]. Use an extra-fine abrasive bullet to buff and polish the inside edge of each ring [G]. Correctly soldered seams should be invisible.

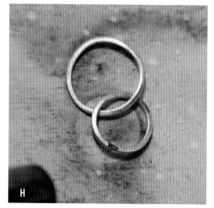

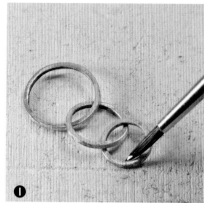

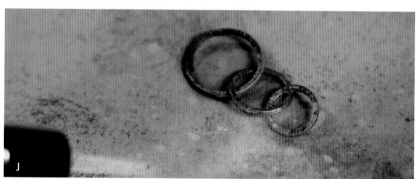

9mm ring **[H]**. Quench, pickle, rinse, and dry. Remove any excess solder.

Attach a 7mm ring to each 9mm soldered ring in the same way. Apply a pallion of easy solder to each seam **[I]**. Solder the seams closed **[J]**. Quench, pickle, rinse, and dry.

Make two wire bars and attach them to the linked rings

Cut two 15mm pieces of 18-gauge sterling silver square wire (about as long as the outside diameter of the 12mm ring). Use chainnose pliers to straighten each piece of wire and a needle file to make the ends flat and square. Use 320-grit sandpaper to sand all the surfaces.

Hold the 7mm ring on the edge of a bench block. Use the flat side of a needle file to file a flat spot on the outer edge of the ring at the solder seam **[K]**. Repeat for the other 7mm ring. Sand both sides of each 7mm ring to remove any burrs.

Make two stacks of ceramic solder board pieces or small charcoal block pieces. Place the 7mm ring on the top edge of the top board so the ring lies flat with the filed, flat spot exposed and facing to the right. Hang the other rings down between the stack of blocks.

Flux the exposed flat edges of the ring and the bar. Position the fluxed side of the bar flush with the filed flat spot of the ring. Place an easy solder pallion at the far side of the seam between the ring and the bar **[L]**.

Solder the 9mm rings closed

Attach a 9mm ring to each of the 12mm soldered rings. Make sure that the ends of the 9mm rings are flush. Position the linked rings on the solder board with the seams of the 9mm rings as far as possible from the seams of the larger rings.

Following the same steps as you did for the 12mm rings, apply and dry flux, place a piece of medium solder at the inside edge of each 9mm ring, and heat until the solder flows and fills the seam of each

Initially focus the flame on the linked rings to bring all the metal up to soldering temperature. Solder the wire and ring by holding the flame in front of the ring to pull the solder forward through the seam **[M]**. When the flux starts to clear, focus the flame over the solder and the bar. After the solder flows, quench, pickle, rinse, and dry. Repeat to solder the other bar and linked rings.

Use flush cutters to trim the ends of each bar so the ends are square. Use sandpaper and abrasive wheels to smooth and round the edges of each bar. Use abrasive wheels to clean any oxidation and solder from the rings.

Make and attach posts

Cut two 1.5cm pieces of 20-gauge round sterling silver wire. Use a needle file to make both ends flat and square. Roll the wire pieces between two metal bench blocks to straighten and stiffen the wire. Place a piece of 320-grit sandpaper on a metal bench block. Sand one end of each wire across the sandpaper to smooth and flatten it. The end must be perfectly flat to make a solid solder join with the earring bar. Use sandpaper to remove any oxidation from the sides of each wire.

Clean and cut some pallions of extra-easy solder. (Because this join will be hidden from view, these pallions can be slightly larger than the ones used to solder the rings.) Place the back of the bar and 7mm ring on the two stacks of solder blocks to allow the larger rings to hang down between the blocks. Lightly heat and apply flux to the bar. Heat until dry.

Place the post flat side down in the end of the third hand tweezers. The wire needs to be suspended as straight as possible. Arrange to allow the bottom of the wire to press firmly down onto the middle of the bar back.

Pick up a piece of extra-easy solder with a paintbrush dipped in flux. Place the pallion at the back of the vertical post. Lightly heat the flux to dry. Heat the metal jaws of the third hand tweezers with the torch for 10–15 seconds **[N]**. Move the torch to the front of the rings and heat the ceramic block and the rings. When

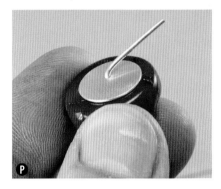

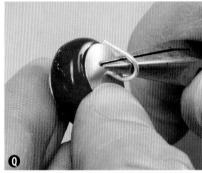

the flux starts to clear, focus the flame at the front base of the post until the solder pulls forward through the seam **[O]**. Allow to cool briefly. Pick up with tweezers, quench, pickle, rinse, and dry. Repeat to attach the other post.

Finish the earrings

Trim the end of the earring wires to 1–1.5cm. Use an abrasive wheel, polishing paper, or a cup bur to file and smooth the ends. Clean any residual solder and oxidation with abrasive wheels. Give each disk a satin finish by buffing with a piece of 400-grit polishing paper held over a metal bench block.

If you are using dyed coral beads, apply a thin coat of microcrystalline wax to set the color. When dry, buff to a high polish with a paper towel. Pick out any wax left in any cracks with a needle.

Pass a balled wire through a domed disk, coral bead and a second domed disk. Hold the assembly tight against the balled wire and fold the wire straight over to nearly a 90-degree angle **[P]**. Continue to form a round wire loop by bending the wire around the pliers in a U shape **[Q]**. Trim the excess wire and string one of the 12mm rings on the loop. Use an abrasive wheel or piece of sandpaper to buff the end of the wire smooth, and then push the end of the wire down toward the disk to complete the connection. Use an extra-fine abrasive wheel to buff out any nicks. Repeat to finish the other earring. Wash the earrings in a soapy water solution, rinse, and dry. ■

RIVETED BEACH STONE
bracelet

You will drill a large hole in each stone as the setting for a large tube rivet. You'll also learn how to solder chain ends on sterling silver beaded chain. This is a handy technique to master, allowing you to buy chain in bulk and make customized length chains with clasps. As embellishment, add a few textured sterling silver charms cut from silver sheet.

TOOLKITS
• Drilling
• Torchwork
• Cutting
• Filing
• Tube-Riveting
• Finishing
• Forming & Forging
• Antiquing

ADDITIONAL TOOLS & SUPPLIES
• Water dish
• Small wood blocks (to fit inside water dish)
• Drafting templates (squares and ovals)
• Rotary tumbler (optional)

MATERIALS
• Fine-silver tubing, 6.3mm outer diameter (4cm)
• 3mm sterling silver bead chain (15.5–16cm)
• 2 sterling silver chain end caps (3mm)
• Sterling silver or fine-silver sheet, 20- or 22-gauge (2.5x8cm)
• Sterling silver lobster-claw clasp (2cm with attached jump ring)
• 14-gauge fine-silver or sterling silver wire (10–12cm)

BEADS
• Assortment of thin beach stones, 3–4mm thick, 1.5x2cm

DESIGN NOTE
The stones I used are thin basalt from Lake Superior. You can use stones from a beach or river in your area, but test-drill one first—some stones will be difficult to drill because of their mineral composition.

FInished length: 20.5cm

Drill the stones

The stones used in this project are about
3mm thick. Thinner stones can be used,
but you risk cracking them during the
rivet-setting process. Use an ultra-fine-
point marker to mark a spot at least 3mm
from the edge to drill the hole.

Set the drilling position

Dip the stone in water and place it on a
flat, stable surface. Hold the rotary tool
vertically, place the end of the 6.5mm
hollow core bit squarely on top of the
mark, and slowly start the rotary tool.
Drill for a few seconds only—just long
enough to start to create or set the hole
with the bit [A]. The drill bit might jump
around initially. Use a firm grip on the
rotary tool and brace your forearm on
the bench surface to help stabilize the
drilling process.

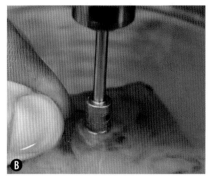

Drill the stone hole

Place a small wood block inside a small
dish. (You also can use a stack of blocks.)
The block should be nearly as tall as the
height of the dish. Place the stone on top
and add water to barely cover the top of
the stone. Hold the stone in place and
place the drill bit in position. Slowly bring
the rotary tool to a comfortable speed
and hold the bit firmly on the stone. The
water acts as a lubricant and flushes
out the stone debris [B]. It also keeps
the stone and drill bit from overheating.
Continue drilling the stone underwater
until you feel the wood block catch the bit
as it emerges from the other side of the
stone. Repeat the process with the second
stone. Occasionally you'll need to remove
a stone plug from the drill bit: Poke a
needle through the base opening or the
side holes to pry it out.

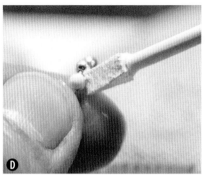

Anneal and size the tubing

See the tube-riveting exercise on p. 28 for
instructions on how to set tube rivets. Set
a rivet in each of the stones. I made two
tube-riveted stones for my bracelet [C].

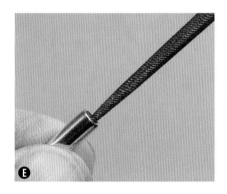

Prepare the bead chain

Cut 15.5–16cm of 3mm sterling silver
bead chain. Buff the outer half of each end
bead using 400-grit polishing paper to
remove any oxidation. Although pickling
is not absolutely necessary, placing the
chain in warm pickle for a few minutes
will ensure that it is totally clean. Rinse
and dry.

This step is optional, but for extra
assurance that the solder does not flow
up and fuse the two end beads, apply
anti-flux to the second-to-last bead [D].
Allow to dry.

Prepare the chain end caps

Check the fit of the end caps with the two
end beads on the chain: Each end bead
should fit into an end cap. Use a round
needle file to file the inside lip of each
cap [E]. Sand the base of each end cap

to remove any oxidation. Place the caps
in pickle, rinse, and dry thoroughly to be
sure no water remains in the cap—it could
bubble up when heated and disturb the
solder placement.

Prepare the solder pallions

Sand the solder wire before cutting to
remove any oxidation. Prepare 4–8 small
extra-easy solder pallions.

Prepare the soldering setup

I like to use broken pieces of honeycomb
ceramic board on top of my solder board
to support each end cap, open side up [F].
You can also prop a cap by setting its end
in the hole or notch of a small steel cotter
pin. Heat the cap very lightly and apply a
light coating of flux. Continue to heat until
the flux turns powdery white.

DESIGN NOTE

I made this bracelet 3cm larger than my wrist, measured just above my wrist bone. One or two jump rings can be used for the bracelet. The small jump ring shown in the project photo was provided with the lobster-claw clasp. This project can be converted into a necklace by using a longer chain. Set smaller tube rivets if you use fine chain.

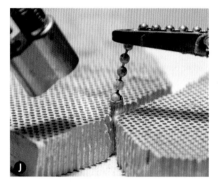

Place the end of a third hand tweezers directly over the end cap. Lower the end bead onto the cap, making sure the two pieces have good contact [G]. Drape the remainder of the chain along the top of the third hand to keep it out of the way. Adjust the height of the third hand to make sure that the second-to-last chain bead is not touching the end bead.

Heat the end cap and the last few chain beads and apply a light coating of flux. Spray some flux on the chain draped along the top of the third hand to protect the chain from oxidation. Continue heating until the flux dries. Make sure you can see dried flux on the lowest chain bead and on the edge of the end cap.

Apply the solder pallions

Dip a fine-tip paintbrush in flux, dab off the excess flux, and pick up a solder pallion. Place a pallion on the left rear and right rear sides of the exposed half of the chain bead. Each pallion should be in contact with both the bead and the lip of the end cap [H].

Preheat the third hand

Use the tip of the torch flame to heat the tip of the third hand for 3–4 seconds [I]. Avoid pointing the torch flame directly at the chain.

Solder the chain and end caps

Use the tip of the torch flame to preheat the ceramic board below the cap [J]. Move the flame tip back and forth around the cap. Hold the torch low and bring the flame tip closer to the bead cap for a few seconds [K]. Brush the flame tip across the cap a few times.

When the powdery white flux turns clear, brush the flame quickly up and down the chain beads once and focus the flame again on the front of the chain cap. When the solder flows, quickly remove the torch. Allow the assembly to cool for a few seconds. The third hand will be hot, so be careful when removing the chain. Quench, pickle, rinse, and dry. Check the solder join. Solder the other end of the chain to the second chain end.

SAFETY Polishing chain with a rotary tool can be dangerous. Use a very slow speed and wear eye protection. In this project, focus on polishing only the end caps. Grasp the attached chain very tightly and keep it out of the path of the spinning wheel. An option is to use a rotary tumbler and tumble-polish the chain.

Polish the end caps

When you use a spinning wheel near chain, make sure you are holding the chain very tightly to prevent it from wrapping around the spinning mandrel and wheel. Fold over the end of the chain and hold the end tightly. Use an extra-fine abrasive wheel to remove any residual solder [L]. Round off the cap base so it blends well with the round ball. Use a 400-grit bristle disk to buff off any oxidation on the end cap [M].

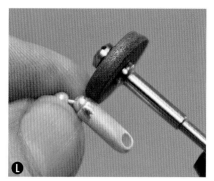

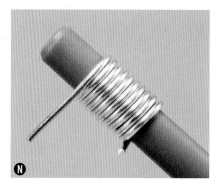

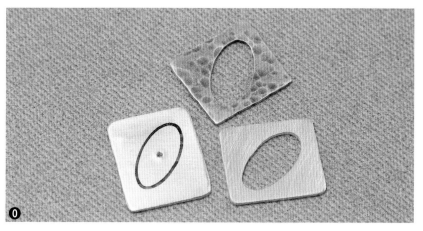

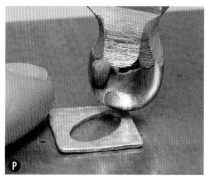

Make the jump rings

Wrap 12cm of 14-gauge fine-silver wire around a 8 or 9mm diameter mandrel to make rings with an outer diameter of approximately 11mm **[N]**. (I used a plastic pen casing as a mandrel.) Saw the rings apart using a 3/0 saw blade. Sand the cut ends with 400-grit silicon carbide sandpaper to remove any burrs. (You'll have extra jump rings; you need just one or two for this bracelet.)

Saw the silver charms

Using drafting templates, trace three squares, approximately 15–17mm wide, onto 20-gauge fine-silver sheet. The shapes do not need to be exactly the same size. Saw out the shapes. Use an oval drafting template to trace a 1cm-long oval in the center of each square. Drill a hole in the oval with a #60 drill bit. Place a 2/0 or 3/0 saw blade through the drilled hole, mount the blade in the saw, and saw out the oval. This image shows a square with a drill hole pierced, one with the oval sawed out, and one square that has been textured and antiqued **[O]**.

Use the flat face of a hand file around the outer edges of the squares to remove imperfections. Use the curved side of a half-round file to smooth any imperfections in the oval. Sand the squares on 400-grit silicon carbide sandpaper to remove the edge burrs. Use an extra-fine-grit abrasive bullet to polish the inner edges of the oval cutout. Use an extra-fine-grit wheel to polish and bevel the outer edges of the squares.

Texture the silver charms

Texture both sides of each silver charm with the ball-peen end of a chasing hammer **[P]** or a texturing hammer. Sand both sides of each charm with 400-grit polishing paper.

Antique the charms

Antique the charms with liver of sulfur. Rinse and dry. Buff both sides of each charm with super-fine steel wool to highlight the texture.

Assemble and finish the bracelet

String the charms between the two riveted stones onto the chain. Attach a 14-gauge wire jump ring onto one of the chain end caps. Close the ends of the jump ring so they are flush. Attach the lobster-claw clasp to the other end cap. ∎

COLLECTOR'S
necklace

This pendant is a showcase for some of your favorite beads. In this project, you'll solder end caps to sterling silver snake chain. I'll teach you a trick for keeping the solder from flowing into the fine, interwoven chain links and preventing the links from fusing together.

Don't care to solder? Simply use a finished necklace chain.

TOOLKITS
- Drilling
- Cutting
- Finishing
- Torchwork
- Forming & Forging
- Filing

ADDITIONAL TOOLS & SUPPLIES
- Single-edge razor blade

MATERIALS
- 26-gauge sterling silver sheet for 12mm disk (1.5x1.5cm)
- 16-gauge fine-silver wire for connectors (14cm)
- 16-gauge sterling silver wire (12cm)
- 18-gauge fine-silver wire (6cm)
- 1.5mm sterling silver snake chain (45–60cm) or a finished necklace chain with clasps
- 2 1.5–2mm sterling silver chain end caps
- Sterling silver lobster-claw clasp and jump ring

BEADS
- Assortment of beads from about 2–8mm (see "Select the beads")

Finished width (pendant): 7.5cm

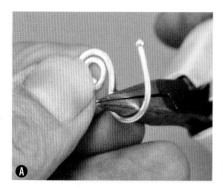

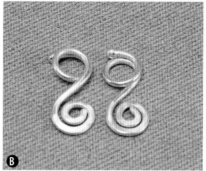

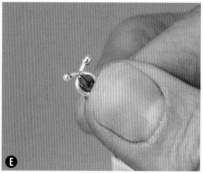

Select the beads

Choose a series of beads that are graduated in size. In the final pendant, the largest bead will be in the center and sizes will get smaller toward the ends. Notice that the beads are not placed symmetrically from left to right, and a silver spacer was added between the turquoise pumpkin bead and the amber disk. If the beads you choose do not fit onto 16-gauge wire, enlarge the holes by drilling underwater.

Prepare a silver spacer disk

Use a disk cutter to cut a 12mm disk. Drill a hole in the center with a #52 high-speed twist drill bit. Smooth the top of the disk with 400-grit polishing paper.

Make two figure-8 connector loops

Cut two 7cm pieces of 16-gauge fine-silver wire. Make sure your micro torch is freshly charged with gas (or use a jumbo butane torch) and ball one end of each wire. On the other end of each wire, make a two-revolution spiral with a center opening of about 3mm and an outside diameter of about 1cm. Use a chasing hammer to forge the spirals. Buff with an extra-fine abrasive wheel.

Hold the chainnose pliers or a narrow mandrel against the wire above the spiral to form the start of a figure-8 that will be about 2cm long [A]. (If any of your beads have a diameter greater than 2cm, make the figure-8 connectors a bit taller to make sure the necklace chain does not touch the beads.)

Continue to wrap the balled end of the wire around the pliers or mandrel into a coil. Wrap the wire around the mandrel, keeping the end toward the left side of the connector. Form a second connector with a coiled end that mirrors the first (wraps to the right). Note that the base spirals match [B]. Buff each connector with polishing paper or tumble-polish.

Prepare the bead bar

Arrange the beads and the two figure-8 connectors on a 12cm piece of 16-gauge sterling silver wire. Position each connector so the balled end points to the front and is several beads (about 1.5–2cm) from the end of the bead arrangement. Adjust the arrangement as necessary and center it on the wire. Mark the outer edge of each end bead on the wire. Remove the beads and connectors.

Forge the bead bar

Bending by hand, make a slight curve in the wire. Use a chasing hammer to gently forge the wire to add some stiffness. Don't overflatten the wire or the beads won't fit over the wire. Trim both ends, leaving about 12mm of wire beyond the marker lines. File the ends smooth. Use a chasing hammer to forge one end into a paddle shape [C]. Do not forge past the mark. Center the bead arrangement with connectors on the wire. Mark the outer edge of each end bead on the wire. At this point you should still be able to slide the beads up the wire toward the paddle end.

Use a chasing hammer to forge the other end of the wire into a paddle [D]. Hold the wire flat so both paddles lie in the same plane. Sand off the marker lines. Use an extra-fine abrasive wheel to buff and round off the paddle ends until they are uniform and smooth.

Finish the pendant

Cut two 3cm pieces of 18-gauge fine-silver wire. Make a small ball on both ends of each wire. Wrap each balled-end wire into a loop around the end of the chainnose pliers' jaws [E].

Center the beads and connectors on the bead bar again. Place a wire loop next to the last bead on each end of the bead bar. Use your fingers to tighten the loop around the bar.

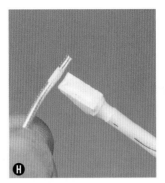

When the wire becomes too stiff and small to handle, use chainnose pliers to squeeze a loop into a tight coil around the bead bar [F]. After several revolutions, make sure the beads are in position and push down on the balled ends with chainnose pliers to secure them around the bar [G]. Repeat on the other end of the bar with the second wire loop, tightening the loop against the end bead as you wrap the balled wire ends around the bar. Use an extra-fine knife-edge abrasive wheel to buff off any nicks in the wire. Use a 400-grit polishing stick to buff the paddles until they are uniform.

Prepare the solder, chain, and end caps for soldering

Prepare some extra-easy or easy silver solder pallions. To remove any oxidation from the snake chain, use an extra-fine abrasive wheel to lightly buff around the last 5mm of each end. Prevent the solder from flowing into the chain links by applying a band of anti-flux around the chain 5mm past the chain end [H]. Do not get any fluid on the last 5mm of chain.

The end caps are about 6mm long. They are not a solid tube; they fold in half down the length. Use a round needle file to rough up the inside of each cap. Use a fine-tip paintbrush to apply some liquid flux to the inside of the caps near the

base. Place the caps on a solder board or charcoal block and lightly heat the caps with a butane torch to dry the flux. Cool.

Solder the chain and end caps

Place an end cap onto one end of the chain. Use chainnose pliers to crimp the base of each end tightly around the end of the chain. Make sure you can feel the chain rubbing on the inside of the cap. To improve the contact, you can also lightly flatten the end of the chain with a chasing hammer to widen it to better fit the end cap. Place the chain on a charcoal block with the length of the chain extending off the block. The chain should be parallel to the front of the block.

Place a single-edge razor blade across the chain so the edge of the blade is just below the base of the chain end, covering the dried anti-flux. Using flux on a fine-tip paintbrush, pick up and place two pallions at the base of the cap, one pallion on the far side, and another near you [I], all in contact with the chain. There is no need to use a wide application of flux, which might encourage the solder to flow the wrong way onto the chain.

Use the tip of the butane torch flame to preheat both edges of the razor blade for about 10–15 seconds [J]. Do not place the flame tip anywhere near or down the

length of the chain; heat only the edges of the blade. Hold the flame at the front of the block, pointing across the end cap [K]. For a few seconds, heat the charcoal block at the edge of the cap. Bring the flame end closer and pulse it across the cap for a few seconds. The cap will start to glisten. When it turns a dull red and the solder flows, remove the flame. Pick up the chain with tweezers and quench.

Check to see if the end cap has soldered. With this type of cap, occasionally one side will not solder. If necessary, set up the chain and razor blade and apply a new solder pallion and solder again as described above. Repeat for the other chain end with the other end cap. Quench the chain. Pickle only the soldered ends of the chain for 10 minutes, rinse, and dry. Polish the end caps and chain end by holding the end in a small, tight loop and using a 400-grit bristle disk at low speed.

Buff the chain end caps

Use an abrasive wheel to smooth and bevel the side seam and base of the cap for a clean look [L]. Use a polishing cloth or tumble-polish the chain if desired.

Assemble the necklace

String the chain through the connectors. Attach a lobster-claw clasp to one end and a jump ring to the other. ■

SOLDERED LINK
necklace

This project introduces you to making a soldered-link chain. You'll cut large rings, solder them closed, and then turn them into ovals. The ovals are linked by small, coiled-wire connectors. The large-hole beads are suspended on balled-end wire that repeats the motif of the connectors. This design works well for large, irregularly shaped beads.

TOOL NOTE
A micro butane torch can be used for all the soldering steps, but use a jumbo torch to ball the ends of the 14-gauge wire.

TOOLKITS
• Forming & Forging
• Cutting
• Filing
• Finishing
• Torchwork

ADDITIONAL TOOLS
• Combination flatnose/half-round pliers

MATERIALS
• 14-gauge fine-silver wire (100cm)
• 16-gauge fine-silver wire (140cm)

BEADS
• 6 semiprecious stone beads,
  1.75–2.75cm

DESIGN NOTE
My beads are apatite, chrysophrase, and recycled glass.

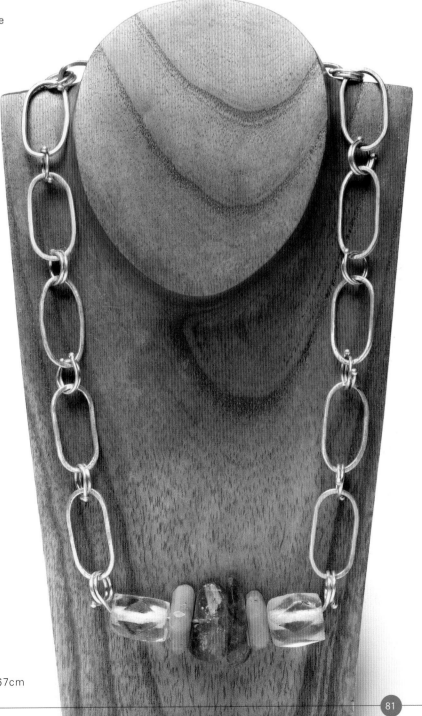

Finished length: 67cm

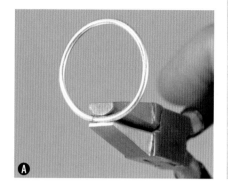

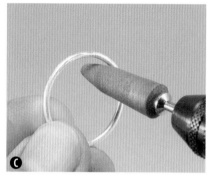

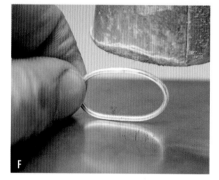

Make the fine-silver rings

I used two sizes of wood dowels to form the large rings: 15mm and 19mm in diameter. Form the rings from fine-silver wire: two 14-gauge at 15mm, 14 14-gauge at 19mm, and one 16-gauge at 15mm. Cut three or four rings at a time using a jeweler's saw. (You may end up with extras.) The ends must be perfectly flush. If they are not flush, file them with a needle file. Sand both ends with 320-grit silicon carbide sandpaper to remove the edge burr. One trick that makes this easy is to fold a 1x4" piece of the sandpaper in half to make a 1x2" sheet. Run this small sheet back and forth inside the join to remove the burrs. Use combination flatnose/half-round pliers to make the ends flush and form the ring [A].

Solder the rings

Prepare some hard silver solder pallions, which will be the best color match to hide the seams. Place the rings on a solder board with the seams in front. Preheat each ring lightly and add a light coating of flux. Heat the rings until the flux dries. Place a pallion at the back inside edge of each ring at the seam [B]. Heat the ring. When the flux starts to clear, move the flame to the front of each ring to pull the solder forward through the seam. When finished, use tweezers to flip each ring over and reheat from directly above

to pull the solder up through the seam. This double-heating trick will help the solder flow uniformly through the seam. If the ends are soldered but there is still a small gap in the seam, add another hard solder pallion and reheat. Solder each ring closed in this way. Quench, pickle, rinse, and dry. Use an extra-fine abrasive wheel to clean up any solder on the outside edges of each ring. Use an extra-fine abrasive bullet to remove any excess solder on the inside of each seam [C].

Form the rings into oval links

Place a ring over the open jaws of a pair of roundnose pliers with the solder seam (shown by the dot) 90 degrees from each jaw [D]. Slowly open the pliers to form the oval. Use a round mandrel to curve the oval ends if they became too pointed [E]. Adjust the contour of each link with a rawhide mallet until the two long sides

are parallel [F]. Use the half-domed face of a chasing hammer in soft, outward strikes to make each link uniformly flat [G]. The wire should be about 1mm wide. The large oval links should be about 28–30mm long and 15–16mm wide. The three small links should be about 22–23mm long and 12–13mm wide.

Sand and polish the links

Use 320-grit sandpaper to smooth both sides of each link. If your bench block has nicks, protect the links by placing a piece of paper under the link and sanding with a sanding stick [H]. Use an extra-fine abrasive wheel to polish the outside of each link and a bullet shape to polish the inside. Use the wheel to bevel the outside and inside edges of each link [I]. Use 400-grit polishing paper to smooth both flat sides of each link.

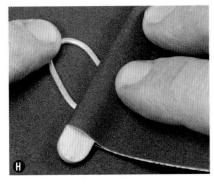

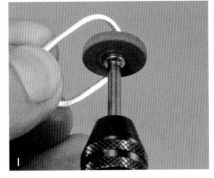

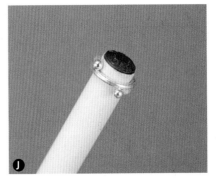

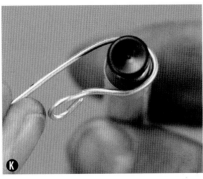

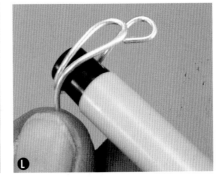

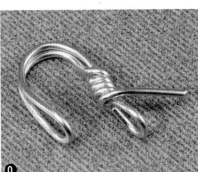

Prepare the connectors

Cut 16 6cm pieces of 16-gauge fine-silver wire. Use a jumbo butane torch to a make a small ball on both ends of each wire. Wrap each wire around an 8mm diameter mandrel about 1½ times **[J]** (I used a ballpoint pen as a mandrel).

Form the wrapped wire clasp

Make a simple loop (for the base of clasp) in one end of a 12cm piece of 16-gauge fine-silver wire. The loop should be large enough to allow one of the connectors to move around easily when connected. Form the top of the clasp over a round, 9–10mm diameter mandrel **[K]**.

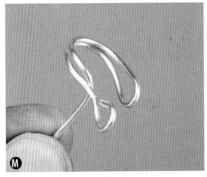

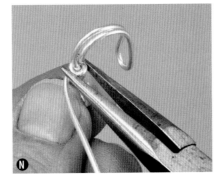

Extend the wire about 25mm, nearly to the bottom of the simple loop, and bend it 180 degrees **[L]**. At the midpoint of the clasp, bend the wire 90 degrees **[M]**. If the wire is getting difficult to handle at this point, anneal it to add flexibility. Wrap the wire around the neck of the clasp, coiling downward **[N]** about 3–5 times **[O]**. Trim the excess wire and use pliers to press the wire end flush with the coil. Make an inward bend in the nose of the clasp. Use an extra-fine abrasive wheel to polish out any marks.

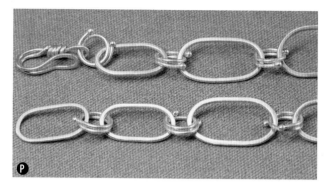

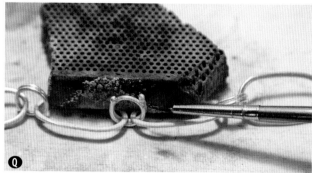

Assemble the chain

Open all of the coiled wire connectors by spreading the balled wire ends just far enough away from the main coil to allow an oval link to slide in. Use connectors between components and attach them in this order for the first side of the necklace: clasp, 15mm 14-gauge link, and seven 19mm 14-gauge links [P]. On the opposite side, start with a 15mm 16-gauge link and add a 15mm 14-gauge link and seven 19mm 14-gauge links.

Solder the connectors

Close each connector and make sure that both balled wire ends are in contact with the coil. Prepare some medium solder pallions. Place two connected oval links flat on the soldering surface. Lean the coiled wire connector with the balled ends pointing upward against a solder board. Heat the connector with the torch flame and apply flux to the connector. Heat again until dry.

Dip a fine-tip paintbrush in flux and place a medium solder pallion at the seam between each ball and the coil [Q]. Apply some heat to the two closest oval links and the base of the connector coil. After the flux turns clear, move the flame higher to the balled connector ends until the solder flows. Do not drop the flame down toward the flat oval links; keep the flame near the balled wire ends to prevent the solder from flowing down to the links. Move down the chain to solder the next connector in the same way until all the connectors have been soldered.

Clean the links and connectors

Use an extra-fine abrasive knife-edge wheel to remove any solder on the connectors. Smooth with a 200- or 400-grit bristle disk. Clean the links with 320-grit silicon carbide sandpaper or 400-grit polishing paper. Use a small polishing stick to clean the inside of each link.

Enlarge the bead holes

Check the fit of the beads on the 16-gauge wire. Depending on the hardness of the semiprecious stone beads, a thin, tapered diamond bit might be enough to enlarge the hole. If not, use a 1.5–2mm hollow-core diamond bit. Drill underwater with the rotary tool plugged into a GFCI outlet.

Prepare the bead bar

The length of my beads as strung on the wire is 7cm. Cut a piece of 16-gauge fine-silver wire equal to the length of the bead arrangement plus 14cm. Lightly forge the center 5–6cm of the wire with a chasing hammer. With your fingers, add a very slight bow to this center section as well. String the beads onto the wire.

You will need two pairs of metal tweezers to hold the wire and beads for balling the wire. Use one pair to hold one wire end vertically in the torch flame and the second as support to keep the beads away from the flame. Ball the wire end. Repeat on the opposite end of the wire. Allow the wire to cool. Center the beads on the wire and mark the outer edge of each end bead on the wire. Coil each balled end toward each outer bead using an 8mm mandrel (the same as you used to make the coiled wire connectors) [R]. Make the coils mirror images so the ball is at the front of each coil.

Finish the beaded pendant

Use chainnose pliers to bend each coil 90 degrees so the balled ends face forward [S]. Gently open each coil enough so you can slide in the end link of each chain half. Press the coils closed with pliers. ■

ABACUS *CHARM* *bracelet*

This project can be used to feature your favorite lampwork glass beads, separated by sterling silver spacers that are etched on both sides. The beads and spacers can slide freely on the snake chain. Four styles of sterling chain are used in this design.

TOOLKITS
- Cutting
- Forming & Forging
- Filing
- Finishing
- Torchwork
- Etching (ferric nitrate)
- Drilling
- Antiquing

ADDITIONAL SUPPLIES
- Drafting templates (squares and circles)
- Extra solder boards or pieces
- Rotary tumbler (optional)

MATERIALS
- 12-gauge sterling silver wire (4cm)
- 14-gauge fine-silver wire (5.25cm)
- 14-gauge sterling silver round wire (7cm)
- 16-gauge fine-silver wire (40cm)
- 22-gauge sterling silver sheet (5x5cm)
- Sterling silver chain in four styles (13cm each): 2–2.5mm diameter snake chain, 2.5mm diameter beaded chain, long-link chain (10mm links), and short-link chain (5mm links)
- 2–2.5mm sterling silver chain end caps (4)

BEADS
- Lampwork glass beads with a minimum 2mm hole (4)

Make the toggle clasp

Cut 4cm of 12-gauge sterling silver wire. With your fingers, form a slight curve in the wire. Lightly forge the ends into paddle shapes with a chasing hammer. The wire will lengthen slightly. Trim it to 4cm long. Use a hand file to smooth off the ends and an extra-fine abrasive wheel to smooth the wire. Cut a 5.25cm piece of 14-gauge fine-silver wire. Use a jumbo butane torch to ball each end of the wire. The length should be about 4.5cm at this point. Mark the middle of the wire and bend it around a pen to form an open-ended C shape. Start to coil the end of the balled wire over the top of the bar as shown, right **[A]**. Coil the other end of the beaded wire in the opposite direction under the bar. Leave a 3mm gap between the center of the coiled wire and the bar so a thick jump ring can be attached later. Slide the balled wire off the bar. Use chainnose pliers to wrap each end into a tight coil **[B]**, keeping the ends open. Use an extra-fine abrasive wheel to buff

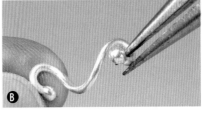

Finished length: 20.5cm

off any marks. Slide the bar back in place within the coiled wire. Use chainnose pliers to tighten each balled end around the bar **[C]**. The coiled wire should fit tightly enough so the bar doesn't move. Smooth the toggle bar with an extra-fine abrasive wheel to remove any marks.

Prepare the connectors

Cut five 5cm pieces of 16-gauge fine-silver wire. Ball both ends of all the wires. Wrap four wires around an 8mm diameter mandrel **[D]**, and wrap one wire around a 6mm mandrel. Open the rings slightly by spreading the overlapped coils.

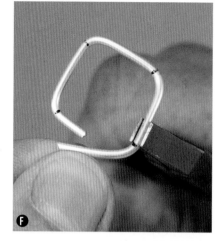
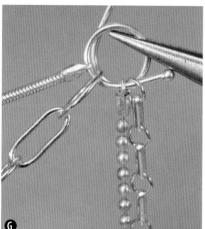

Solder the toggle bar and connectors

(See the Soldered Link Necklace, p. 81, for instructions on making soldered connectors.) Use hard solder to solder the bar to both ends of the balled wire. Connect one of the 8mm connector rings to the toggle bar. Press the coiled wire to make tight contact for a solder join. Use a second solder board to support the ring you are soldering. Place the connector ring on the top board with the other metal pieces hanging over the side of the upper board. Use hard solder to solder the first ring closed. Keep the torch flame focused on the ring you are soldering **[E]**. Let it cool.

Connect a second 8mm ring to the first using hard solder. Arrange the first soldered ring so the soldered join is not touching any metal in case the solder flows when reheating. To help prevent that, heat only the toggle bar and first ring briefly. Quench, pickle, rinse, and dry. Use an extra-fine knife-edge abrasive wheel to remove excess solder.

Form the square toggle ring

Cut 7cm of 14-gauge sterling silver wire. File one end of the wire flat. Use a flatnose pliers to make a 90-degree bend about 6mm from the wire end. Make another mark about 12.5mm from the first corner and make a second bend. Repeat until the fourth corner is formed **[F]**. Cut the wire slightly longer than needed to fit flush against the first end. File until it fits

flush with the first end. Solder the ring closed using hard solder. After pickling, clean up the solder seam using an extra-fine abrasive wheel and bullet. Use a chasing hammer to lightly forge the ring until the surfaces are evenly flattened. The final dimensions of the square toggle ring are approximately 2x2cm.

Solder the connectors to the toggle ring

Use hard solder to connect two 8mm connectors to the square toggle ring as you did for the toggle bar. Make sure the previous solder seams are not touching any metal from an adjoining part. Use an extra-fine abrasive wheel to remove excess solder.

Solder end caps to the chains

Cut a 13mm piece of 2.5mm sterling silver snake chain. Use a needle file to file along the inside walls of the chain end cap. Use the razor blade technique with easy silver solder to solder the end cap to the chain (see the Collector's Necklace,

p. 78, for detailed soldering instructions). Solder an end cap to each end of a 13mm piece of 2.5mm sterling silver bead chain using easy solder (see the Riveted Beach Stone Bracelet, p. 74, for detailed soldering instructions). After pickling the chain ends, use an extra-fine abrasive wheel to remove any excess solder.

Connect the chains to the toggle bar

Cut a 5cm piece of 16-gauge fine-silver wire. Use a butane torch to ball one end of the wire. Leaving the last 5mm of each end straight, wrap the center of the wire around the 8mm mandrel. Spread the coil apart a bit, and string one end of each of the four chains **[G]**.

Ball the other end of the wire, placing the four chains in the tweezers handle and keeping them away from the flame **[H]**. Use caution and avoid touching the chains; heat may transfer to the chains. Quench. Use the 8mm mandrel to finish coiling the balled wire into a ring.

Assemble and solder

Assemble eight metal spacers with large spacers in the middle, graduating to small spacers to the left and right **[K]**. The metal spacers will be strung in pairs on the 2mm snake chain with a glass bead between each pair. Plan the stringing order and add a very slight dome to the spacers so they hug the beads. Assemble the spacers and beads on the snake chain.

Keeping all the beads and the other chains out of the flame, solder an end cap onto the remaining end of the snake chain using medium or easy solder **[L]**. Use an extra-fine abrasive wheel to clean up any excess solder. Pickle only the soldered chain end. Ball one end of a 5cm piece of 16-gauge fine-silver wire, form the wire around the 8mm mandrel, and attach all of the remaining chain ends to the connector ring. Ball the other end of the wire, keeping the chains and beads away from the flame. Attach this connector to the end connector of the toggle ring. Solder the connector closed using extra-easy solder. Remove any excess solder with an extra-fine abrasive wheel.

Prepare the bead dangle

Use a shallow cup of a wood dapping block to dome the dangle spacers. Ball one end of a 8cm piece of 16-gauge fine-silver wire. String a spacer, the bead, and two or three spacers of graduated sizes.

Attach the dangle and finish

String the remaining 6mm connector onto the toggle ring. Solder the connector closed using extra-easy solder. Use an extra-fine abrasive wheel to remove any excess solder.

Attach the dangle to the 6mm connector. String the wire through the connector, grasp the wire above the charms, and form a wrapped loop **[M]**. Smooth any marks in the wire with an extra-fine abrasive wheel. Polish the connectors, chain end, and clasp loop with a felt wheel charged with polishing compound. Wash the bracelet with soapy water, rinse, and dry. ∎

Open the coil slightly and attach it to the second connector of the toggle bar link. Lay this connector ring on the top edge of a ceramic board. Keep the chains, the other connectors, and the toggle bar away from the flame. Use extra-easy solder to solder this third connector closed **[I]**. After pickling, use an extra-fine abrasive wheel to remove any excess solder from the connector. If desired, tumble-polish the chain/toggle bar section and the toggle ring section for about 30 minutes.

Prepare the etched spacers

Saw a 5x5cm square of 22-gauge sterling silver sheet. Sand both surfaces with 400-grit polishing paper. Create a resist pattern on one side of the metal; I used a rubber mat and an ink pad and reinforced it with nail polish **[J]** (the photo shows the nail polish overlay in progress). Follow the etching instructions on p. 25 to etch the silver for 3–4 hours in ferric nitrate solution. Neutralize and clean the silver.

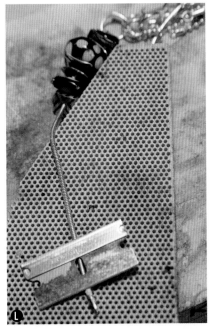

On the nonetched side of the metal, draw 11 or 12 squares and circles of various sizes (10–15mm wide). Saw out the shapes. Set aside 3–4 squares and circles of different sizes for use with the dangle (these do not need to be etched on both sides). Apply a resist design to the non-etched sides of the remaining shapes and coat the etched sides with a layer of nail polish to preserve the etching. Etch, neutralize, and clean the shapes.

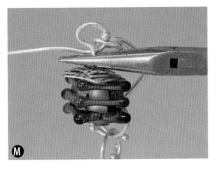

Prepare the spacers for chain

Drill a hole in the center of each spacer (including the dangle spacers) with a #52 high-speed twist drill bit, and drill again with a ³⁄₃₂" drill bit. Polish and bevel the edges of each spacer with an extra-fine abrasive wheel. Antique, smooth with 400-grit polishing paper, and use a polishing cloth to buff the spacers to a high shine. Set aside the 3–4 dangle spacers that were etched on one side only.

BEADED TOGGLE
bracelet

This project features a fabricated, softly textured silver toggle clasp with oval connectors made from square wire. This showpiece clasp is paired with a set of flat, double-drilled beads; I used blue apatite.

TOOLKITS
- Cutting
- Drilling
- Filing
- Finishing
- Torchwork
- Forming & Forging

ADDITIONAL TOOLS
- Combination flatnose/half-round pliers
- Crimping pliers (optional)

MATERIALS
- 22-gauge sterling silver sheet (4x4cm)
- 18-gauge sterling silver square wire (40cm)
- 18-gauge sterling silver wire (3cm)
- 0.021" multistrand beading wire
- 4 sterling silver crimp beads, 1mm
- 4 sterling silver crimp bead covers, 3.2mm
- 4 sterling silver wire guards

BEADS
- 8 square, flat, double-drilled beads, 13mm
- 18 Thai-style silver spacer bars

DESIGN NOTE

If you do not have double-drilled beads, use just one oval ring on each side of the clasp or make it a multistrand bracelet by attaching several strands of small beads to each large ring.

Finished length: 20cm

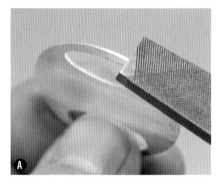

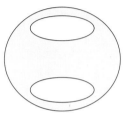

templates

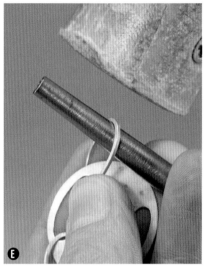

Cut out the toggle clasp pieces

Trace the two templates onto paper or cardstock and transfer the outlines onto 22-gauge sterling silver sheet. Saw the shapes using a 2/0 saw blade. Make a dimple in the center of the two oval cutouts and use a #60 high-speed twist drill bit to drill a hole in each oval. Remove one end of the saw blade from the frame, pass the blade through the hole, reattach the blade in the frame, and saw out the oval. Repeat for the second oval cutout.

File the edges of each piece

Use a hand file to smooth the edges of both metal pieces [A]. Use round and half-round needle files to smooth the edges of the oval cutouts. Sand both sides of each piece on 320-grit silicon carbide sandpaper to remove any burrs. Smooth with 400-grit polishing paper.

Polish the metal edges

Use an extra-fine abrasive bullet to polish the inside edges of the cutouts, and use an extra-fine abrasive wheel to polish the outside edges. Bevel all the cut edges.

Texture and dome the clasp

Use the ball-peen end of a chasing hammer to make dots of texture across the toggle loop part of the clasp. Dome the piece in a shallow cup of a wood dapping block.

Make the oval rings

Anneal 40cm of 18-gauge square sterling silver wire and make at least four jump rings on a 12mm mandrel. Sand the ends with 320-grit silicon carbide sandpaper to remove any burrs. Make sure the ends of each ring are perfectly flush.

Solder the rings to the clasp

Attach two rings to one side of the clasp. Use a combination flatnose/half-round pliers to adjust the ring, making sure the ends are flush and in contact [B]. Solder the rings closed using hard solder [C]. Quench, pickle, rinse, and dry. Use an extra-fine abrasive wheel and bullet to remove any excess solder.

Stretch the rings into ovals

Place a ring at the tips of an open chainnose or roundnose pliers jaws, rotating the solder seam so it is 90 degrees away from the jaws. Slowly open the jaws more to form an oval [D]. Repeat for the other soldered ring. If the rings have slightly pointed ends, place them on a ring mandrel and lightly tap with a rawhide mallet to round the ends [E]. Each ring should be about 12x18mm. Use an extra-fine abrasive bullet to bevel the inner edges of each ring. Smooth each ring with 400-grit polishing paper.

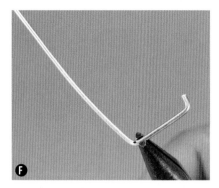

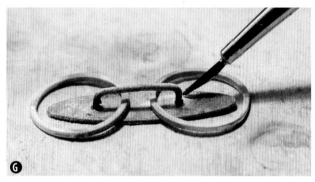

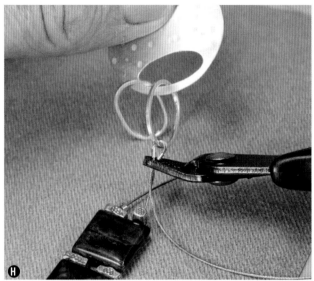

Prepare wire for the toggle bar

Bend the end of a piece of 18-gauge sterling silver wire at a 90-degree angle and make a second right-angle bend 14mm down the wire **[F]**. Trim the end of the wire to make a second 3mm leg. File the bottom of each leg with a flat needle file until the ends are flat.

Solder the toggle bar rings closed

Solder the two remaining rings closed using hard solder. Use an extra-fine abrasive wheel and bullet to remove any excess solder. Shape the rings into ovals.

Solder and finish the toggle bar

Place the oval toggle bar face down on a solder board. Place the bent wire on the back of the bar to check if it can stand upright; if not, file the base of each leg until it is flat and flush with the bar. Place a soldered oval around each leg. Adjust the ovals so their solder seams are not in contact with any part of the bar and the wire is centered on the bar. (A third hand can help here.) Place a large pallion of medium solder at the back of each of the legs **[G]**.

Hold the flame in front of the assembly to pull the solder forward on each leg. After the solder flows, flux the toggle bar, place a second piece of medium solder near the front of each leg, and heat again until the solder flows. Quench, pickle, rinse, and dry.

Remove any oxidation from the back of the toggle bar with a 400-grit bristle disk. Smooth the ovals with a polishing stick.

Assemble the bracelet

Cut two 15cm pieces of 0.021" multistrand beading wire. String the square beads with a silver spacer between each pair. At one end of a wire, string a crimp bead. String the wire through one leg of a wire guard and form the wire guard around one of the clasp rings. String the wire back through the second leg of the guard and back through the crimp bead. Crimp the crimp bead with crimping pliers **[H]**. Trim the excess wire and pull the wire taut against the bead strand. Repeat to add crimp beads and wire guards to the remaining clasp wire and to the two wire ends on the toggle bar end. Cover the crimp beads with crimp covers if desired.

Polish the clasp

Lightly polish the faces of the clasp with 400-grit polishing paper to remove any scratches. ∎

PRONG-SET ROMAN GLASS
ring

This project is ideal for highlighting an irregularly shaped piece: Consider using beach glass, a sparkling drusy, or a pottery shard. I set a gorgeous slab of old Roman glass. A pair of tube rivets secures the ring base to the band.

Finished size:
22x35mm (oval base)

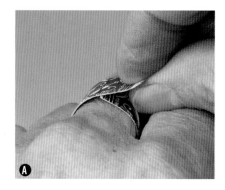

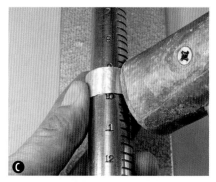

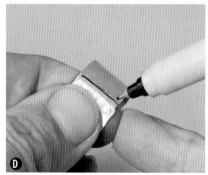

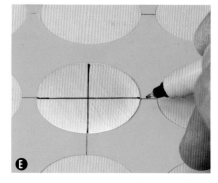

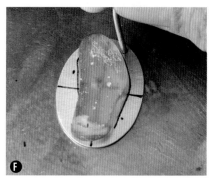

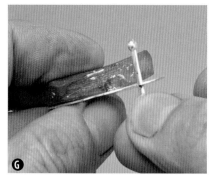

Cut out the band

Cut a 14mm wide ring band template out of cardstock. Start with a template that is 8–8.5cm long and trim as needed; the band should be long enough to wrap around your finger and overlap about 15mm **[A]**. Trace the band onto 24-gauge silver sheet. Saw out the band with a 5/0 or 6/0 saw blade. Sand both sides with 320-grit silicon carbide sandpaper and then 400-grit polishing paper until the surfaces are uniform. Texture the band with a texturing hammer **[B]**. Use a coarse hand file to smooth the sharp corners. Use an extra-fine abrasive wheel to bevel the top and inside edges to make the band comfortable to wear. Smooth both sides with 400-grit polishing paper until the surfaces are uniform.

Form the ring band

Use a set of ring size gauges to determine your ring size. Center the band on a ring mandrel at the position that approximates your ring size. Starting at the center, slowly bend both ends of the band simultaneously around the mandrel. Use a rawhide mallet to continue to form the ring around the mandrel **[C]**. After the band is round, place the ring on your finger and pinch it to a comfortable size. Without relaxing the tension, remove the band and mark the point of overlap **[D]**.

Cut out the oval base

Choose an oval from a drafting template to form the base, allowing a minimum 1mm border when the item to be set is centered on it. My glass cabochon is 15x32mm and my oval is 22x35mm. Trace the oval onto 22- or 24-gauge sterling silver sheet. Saw out the shape with

a 4/0 or 6/0 saw blade. File the edges smooth by filing around the oval in both directions. Sand both sides with 320-grit silicon carbide sandpaper followed by 400-grit polishing paper.

Drill the prong holes in the oval

Use the drafting template's grid to help determine the center of the oval **[E]**. Place the object you are setting on the oval and trace it. Mark four dots around the item to approximate where the prong holes should be drilled. Leave about 1mm between the outside of the tracing and the mark. Place a short piece of 14-gauge

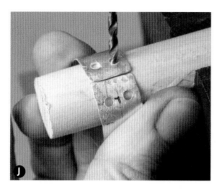

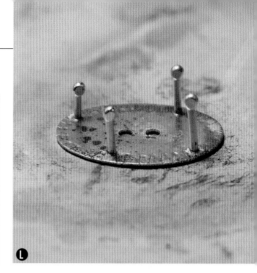

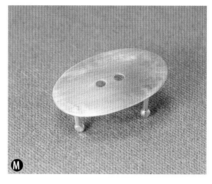

wire on each mark to make sure you left enough room between the object and edge of the oval to allow for the width of the wire **[F]**. Use a #53 high-speed twist drill bit to drill holes at each mark. Sand off the burr on the back of the oval. File the end of a piece of 14-gauge wire flat (you'll use this as a test wire). Smooth the wire end with sandpaper. Use a round needle file to enlarge each hole until the test wire fits tightly.

Stamp the oval
Use design stamps to texture the outer edge of the oval. I used a straight-line stamp and a punch with a tiny domed end. If the oval curls, place it on a bench block and flatten it with a rawhide mallet.

Prepare the prongs
Cut four 25mm pieces of 14-gauge fine-silver wire. (My glass is at most 8mm thick; adjust the length of the wires you cut to be about 12–14mm longer than the thickness of your object.) Ball one end of each wire into a fairly substantial ball. Flatten each ball end with a chasing hammer.

One at a time, place each prong in its position with the balled end about 4mm higher than the object to be set, and mark the prong base where it aligns with the oval **[G]**. Flush-cut the wire. Sand each prong base flat and test that all the prong stems fit in their holes.

Drill the tube rivet holes
Measure the dimensions of your ring band overlap (my overlap was 13x13mm). Mark the dimensions in the middle of the oval and mark the positions for two tube rivets vertically centered in the overlap **[H]**. Use a #53 high-speed twist drill bit to drill a hole. Follow with a 7/64" drill bit to widen each hole. Clean the holes with a round file and enlarge them until the tubing fits snugly.

Drill the ring band holes
On one end of the ring band, mark two holes to match those you marked on the oval. Gently open the band wider and use a 3/32" screw punch to cut out the two holes in the top overlapped section **[I]**. Close the band to the desired size. Use the screw punch to pierce aligned holes in the other end of the band.

Check the fit of the tubing through the sets of holes. If necessary, enlarge the holes with a round needle file. Alternatively, place the band on a 20mm wood dowel locked in the jaws of a bench vice and use a 7/64" drill bit to enlarge the holes **[J]**. You'll still need to enlarge each hole slightly with a round needle file after drilling. Use rolled 320-grit silicon carbide sandpaper to remove burrs on the inside of the band. Test-fit the assembly of the band and the oval threaded with

two pieces of tubing, and use a needle file again if the holes need to be larger. Re-form the band on a mandrel with a rawhide mallet.

Solder the prongs into the oval
Insert the prong stems into the holes with the flattened sides of the ball ends facing the center of the oval. Turn the oval over so the prongs support it. Make sure each prong base is flush with or extending slightly beyond the underside of the oval. Since the prongs may be uneven lengths, you can support the oval at the edge of a solder board. Heat and flux the oval and place a piece of hard solder at the far side of each prong base. Heat the oval. As the flux clears, the solder will flow **[K]**. Using tweezers, flip the oval over and reheat from above to pull the solder to the top of the oval **[L]**. Quench, pickle, rinse, and dry. Use a 400-grit bristle disk to remove excess oxidation from the surface and prongs. On the back of the oval, sand off any excess wire that protrudes until the surface is flush and uniform **[M]**.

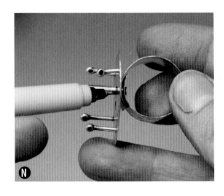

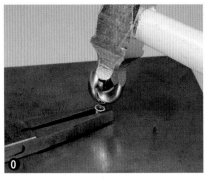

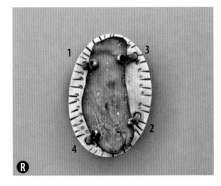

Set the rivets

Anneal a 3cm piece of 2.97mm sterling silver tubing. Sand one end of the tube flat. Insert the sanded end into one of the oval and ring band holes, allowing about 1.5mm to extend on the sanded end. Mark at 1.5mm from the oval surface on the other end **[N]**. Remove the tube and use a tube cutter to cut it at the mark. Cut a second piece of tubing the same size. Sand the ends and edges of the tube.

Hold a tube with flatnose pliers on a metal bench block and use a 3mm center punch to flare the top opening. Use a chasing hammer to roll the collar down around the whole circumference **[O]**. Use an extra-fine abrasive wheel to smooth the rivet collar. Repeat to make a collar at the top of the other tube.

Working from the underside of the band, insert the nonflared end of a tube through the aligned holes in the band. If necessary, enlarge the holes in the ring band with a needle file. Position the oval over the tubes. Place the ring onto the flat nose of a horn anvil. Finish the tube rivet by rolling the collar over with the ball-peen end of a chasing hammer or by striking it with a dapping punch **[P]**. Repeat to rivet the other tube rivet in the other set of holes.

Use an extra-fine abrasive wheel to smooth the rivet flush to the ring band surface. Likewise, the rivet collars on the underside of the ring can be smoothed again with the abrasive wheel.

Antique the oval and ring band

Antique the metal pieces. Bring back the metal highlights with 400-grit polishing paper or superfine steel wool.

Push the prongs over

Position the glass on the oval. Applying pressure starting at the prong base, use the broad side of a flatnose pliers to gently push a prong over the glass **[Q]**. After the prong base and sides contact the glass, gently press the balled end over the glass. After the first prong is pushed into place, follow the order shown to position the remaining prongs **[R]**. ■

SOURCES

Please support your local bead stores, bead shows, and lapidary shops as you assemble your collection of gemstone beads and hand tools. Your local hardware store may carry supplies such as high-speed twist drill bits and silicon carbide sandpaper.

Other supplies and specialty tools for working with metal may be more challenging for you to find; I often rely on online suppliers. I've listed a few of my favorites.

Rio Grande: metal sheet, chains, findings, tools, hollow-core drill bits, high-speed twist drill bits, micron-graded polishing paper, polishing tips in bulk
riogrande.com

Eurotool: hand tools, jewelry pliers, hollow-core drill bits, tube cutters
eurotool.com

Otto Frei: hand tools (including used tools), polishing tips sold singly
ottofrei.com

Radio Shack: ferric chloride etching solution (PCB Etchant Solution)
radioshack.com

ACKNOWLEDGMENTS

Thanks to Lynn Grimm, who shared her knowledge during the 10 years I studied in the metals fabrication workshop at Madison Area Technical College. I would like to thank my Helena Street neighborhood pals Ade, Ann, Kathy, and Mary for allowing me to "practice instruct" them before taking my show on the road. As always, my parents, Gus and Marilyn, deserve credit for instilling the strong farm work ethic that helped me finish this book, and I'm grateful to Aunt Suzanne for sharing her creative energies as well as her turquoise and silver jewelry with me when I was young.

Thanks and credit also go to Mary Wohlgemuth for her suggestion for this book and for her guidance as an editor. I'd also like to thank all the other talented folks at Kalmbach Books for their contribution to this book—especially Lisa Bergman, art director, and photographers Bill Zuback and Jim Forbes for their fine work and helpful advice.

ABOUT THE AUTHOR

KAY RASHKA has been creating jewelry for 25 years, working primarily in sterling silver and semiprecious gemstones. Kay is a scientist in the biotech industry by day and a jewelry artist and instructor by night. "My goal is to help as many people as possible realize how simple sawing metal and soldering can be," she says. "I want to encourage them to create something every day."

Kay teaches in and around her home studio near Madison, Wisconsin, and at venues including the Bead&Button Show, Peninsula School of Art, the Art Glass & Bead Show, and Shake Rag Alley. Her work was featured on the cover of *Art Jewelry* magazine in September 2011. Kay's website is kayrashka.com, she writes a blog at kayrashka.blogspot.com, and you can also find her on Facebook: Kay Rashka Jewelry page.

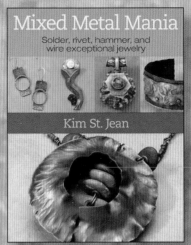